3-2-07

To Roxan

You are one of
big time quotes.

my

I hope you enjoy

The book.

My Best

Richard

MW01025692

Life Zones

Also by Richard Corriere

Going Sane: An Introduction to Feeling Therapy,
1975 (with Joseph Hart and Gerald Binder)

The Dream Makers: Discovering Your Breakthrough Dreams,
1977 (with Joseph Hart)

Psychological Fitness: Twenty-one Days to Feeling Good,
1978 (with Joseph Hart)

Dreaming and Waking: The Functional Approach to Using Dreams,
1980 (with Werner Karle, Lee Woldenberg, and Joseph Hart)

The Functional Analysis of Dreams: A New Theory of Dreaming,
1980 (with Werner Karle, Lee Woldenberg, and Joseph Hart)

Also by Patrick M. McGrady, Jr.

TV Critics in a Free Society, 1959

The Youth Doctors, 1968

The Love Doctors, 1972

The Pritikin Program for Diet and Exercise,
1979 (with Nathan Pritikin)

LIFE ZONES

A Guide to
Finding Your True Self,
Getting On in the Real World, and
Changing Losing Ways into Winning Ways

◆ ◆ ◆

By Richard Corriere, Ph.D.,
and Patrick M. McGrady, Jr.

William Morrow and Company, Inc. / New York

Copyright © 1986 by Richard Corriere, Ph.D., and Patrick M. McGrady, Jr.

All rights reserved. No part of this book may be reproduced or utilized in any form or by any means, electronic or mechanical, including photocopying, recording or by any information storage and retrieval system, without permission in writing from the Publisher. Inquiries should be addressed to Permissions Department, William Morrow and Company, Inc., 105 Madison Ave., New York, N.Y. 10016.

Library of Congress Cataloging-in-Publication Data

Corriere, Richard.
  Life zones.

  Includes index.
  1. Control (Psychology) 2. Self-control.
3. Personality change. 4. Success. I. McGrady,
Patrick. II. Title.
BF632.5.C67 1986   158   85-21733
ISBN 0-688-04480-8

Printed in the United States of America

    2 3 4 5 6 7 8 9 10

BOOK DESIGN BY VICTORIA HARTMAN

This book is dedicated
to my mother and my father
—R.C.

For my three wonderful
children, Ilya, Vanessa, and Ian
—P.M.McG., Jr.

Preface
How to Make This Book Work for You

This book is written for people who want to learn how to perform at their best. I have purposely written short chapters and included lots of learning tests. But if the book is going to work for you, you must work with it by trying out the ideas and doing the exercises.

I have been a personal coach for the past fifteen years. I have spent literally thousands of hours in therapy sessions, workshops, and seminars. I have heard the most bizarre secrets, watched people make the commonest mistakes over and over again, analyzed the nature of relationships, work situations, sex lives, business, and play. I have worked with clients of every description, from severely disturbed schizophrenics to stable, successful individuals.

On hundreds of occasions I would have given almost anything to have a realistic guide for clients of mine, one that would truly assist others, or myself for that matter, to penetrate the fog of life's complexity and get to the bottom of things. How helpful it would have been to have had a *practical* book with a set of principles for analyzing any situation, taking positive action, making important changes, and living a full life. I had hoped for a book that would help people get their act together and take it into the real world.

I had never seen such a book, or even encountered a set of ideas that told people simply and clearly how to make it on their wn in the here and now. Not having found such a book, I decided to write it. *Life Zones* is that book.

Many believe that the way to success and happiness lies in delving deeply into their souls to understand how they got where they are and why they do what they do. But that simply is not true. Success and happiness are not achieved solely by introspection, however profound. They require breaking out of your shell, rediscovering the real world, looking and listening, and trying out what you learn with the people you meet. In the process of dealing with others, you will naturally arrive at a comprehensive perception of your true inner self.

I have ventured into nearly every major school of psychology, explored its tenets and tested its application to human dymanics. Almost all of them talk about effectiveness. *But to be effective you have to change.* This is a book about changes—yours, mine, and those undertaken by people I have known. From my research and practice I have drawn up certain principles that enable me to coach others to change, to put changes of perception into action, and to allow people to prevent others from impeding their progress. Much of this will be new to you. Perhaps even radical. There is a reason for this. A while back I found that I had to break with the antiquated psychological folklore because it posed major hindrances to positive change. Let me list a few of these out-of-date ideas.

To make a change in the present you have to understand the past. Change takes place in the here and now through the actions you take. Once you've taken action, you then have a new, useful perspective on your past. Merely knowing what went wrong in the past will not help you succeed in life.

The personality is fixed. Not true. The personality is exquisitely flexible. Your worst enemy is not mysterious: It is that set of secret rules for failure that you live by. You devised them, and you can scrap them or change them. Once you challenge your status quo, you will be on the way to gaining control over your personality and harnessing your greatest trump card: your innate ability to change.

It's Mom's fault. Mothers have taken a bad rap. Your mother did her job by giving birth to you and keeping your little fingers out of the light sockets and changing your diapers. She was not then, and is not now, responsible for your happiness, fulfillment, or success. You are.

Statistics prove . . . Statistics can say much about groups of people at a particular point in time, but they say little or nothing about you as an individual from one day to the next. Every individual defies statistics, because every individual is unique and has the capacity to change. Your life does not have to reflect what *most* people think or feel. Your life is about you. Period.

I promise you this. If you take the time to read this book carefully and experiment with what you learn, it will help you extract the most out of your leisure, your work, and your relationships. But never forget that this book is about you alone. Do as you will with it. Mark it up. Keep it close to you. Do not lend it out. Make this your own personal handbook for survival and success in the next decade.

Acknowledgments

There is a black woman I have known for the past twenty-five years who deserves special acknowledgment. She is now fifty years old, without a husband, and was down to her last dollar when something special happened to her. She started to try. Her music was nothing less than a driving force behind each word of this book. Tina Turner, thank you for the love, the drive, and the vision of what one can do no matter how far one has fallen.

I also want to acknowledge Bruce Springsteen for music that makes me believe in rock and roll, love, and the goodness of the human spirit. Thanks to the Boss.

On just as serious a note, I want to thank Dr. Ellsworth Baker, who at eighty-two years of age knew more about the human condition, the requirements for change, and resistance to change than any man alive. Dr. Baker, who was the force behind the present-day work of Wilhelm Reich, has kept his faith in human goodness longer than any individual could be expected to. He gave me guidance and knowledge, and I mourn his passing.

I want to acknowledge Dr. Alexander Lowen for his brilliant clinical books, which have taught me something new each time I have read them.

I also want to acknowledge Dr. George Vaillant of Harvard University and Dr. James Lynch of the University of Maryland School of Medicine for their extraordinary research and books that continually prove the wonder of the human spirit.

I want to acknowledge two separate groups of professionals who have influenced me both professionally and personally. In New York City: Dr. George DeLeon who gave me insight and a shoulder to cry on when I desperately needed it; Dr. Jim Frossage of the National Institute for the Psychotherapies, who encouraged me to sustain my vision in psychology; Dr. Michael Friedman, who is one of the best of the human race; and my special friend Henry Beck, Ph.D., who shared his insights concerning the social aspects of the human condition with me. And my dear friend Susan Gray for her vision of what life can be. There is also Carol Bovoso who knows how to reach the heart. In Aspen I want to thank Dr. Kenneth Tutt, Dr. Gerald Alpern, and Dr. Carl Schiller for their support and acceptance, and Dr. Herb Hampshire and Jonathan Stoller for their acceptance, support, and extraordinary human goodness.

In Los Angeles: Judith Light and Robert Desiderio, both of whom proved to be great friends. I thank Craig Kellum and Penny Price for having brought to the world of television a new vision. Anthony Barash, A. Catherine Steel, Wynn Smith, and Larry Watts have given me guidance in diplomacy, patience, and clear thinking.

During the last four years I met two outstanding professionals who were able to help me understand myself and human dynamics in new and exciting ways—Dr. Harvey Stone and Fleur Green, M.A.

Then there are all the great coaches who have been guides in their own ways: John Wooden, Al Maguire, Vince Lombardi, Tommy Lasorda, Leo Durocher, Tom Landry, Vic Braden, Patrick Curry, and all the others too numerous to mention.

This book is the direct result of the patience of three people: Patrick McGrady, Marilyn Abraham of Ballantine Books, and Maria Guarnaschelli of William Morrow and Company. Patrick believed in what I had to say when I felt like giving up. And he added to this book an elegance of style regardless of how I fought him. Marilyn has a sense of humor, insight into human nature, and patience that would have given Job a run for his money. And finally to Maria, who is without a doubt one of the most talented editors alive today.

During the time I needed it most, I found the support of my

mother, Loretta, my father, Joseph, and all my sisters, Joette, Francine, Tina, Marlene, and Regina.

There is not a doubt that this book is here before you because of my wife, Konni, and my daughter, Signe. Their love and encouragement are more than enough to keep me motivated.

And finally I want to acknowledge my clients, who helped me discover what I do best—coach.

Contents

Section Four: Needs—The Personality Fuel 135

Section Five: Images—The Tools of the Personality 159

Section Six: The Right Signals 195

Section Seven: The Four Steps 221

Introduction
Welcome to Sync

Y ou can create your own success. Success comes from making the most of whatever situation you find yourself in. I call that approach to life "Synchrony," or "Sync" for an easier handle. To make the most of any situation, you have to know what is happening outside as well as inside. Success comes when you realize how to put yourself into sync with yourself and your world.

Putting yourself into sync can be achieved through a unique system of situation analysis by determining the "Life Zone" in which you find yourself. Essentially, there are Four Life Zones: Public, Social, Personal, and Intimate. The behavioral regulations for each life zone are different, because the dynamic for each is different; as are the relationships within each zone. The simplicity of this structure will help you to realize quickly how to make the most of each situation.

During my years at the University of California at Irvine, my then graduate adviser and colleague, Joe Hart, and I studied personality theory by turning ourselves into guinea pigs. We wanted to know just how the personality worked. Most of the data we explored were not terribly useful to us, since they dealt largely with abnormal personalities. We wanted some pragmatic insights into ordinary people, not just academic theory about psychiatric cases. After much work, we arrived at a most interesting concept. We found that we could strengthen the personality if we treated it as we might any other part of the body. If we exercised personality, it developed improved tone and performance. If we left it alone, it got out of shape.

Our study showed that the personality is not a fixed system, but a dynamic, changeable entity. The various parts of the personality work much like an automobile engine. When the parts of your engine are in tune, you have a reliable form of transportation. Your car can take you almost anywhere at speeds of your own choosing. When the parts are not in tune, you are overwhelmed with costly repairs and are forced to make other arrangements for transportation. The most distressing part of a car on the rack, or a personality out of commission, is that you are no longer in the driver's seat and no longer have control over when and where you travel.

The central organizing and directing role of the personality belongs to the "self." The self is to the personality what the brain is to the physical body. When the brain is healthy, it has firm control over the body functions. Brain injury, however, can cause loss of control over a number of body functions. It can even cause coma. If the brain dies, the body is as good as dead.

Similarly, if the self is ailing or dead, you no longer exercise control over your personality. Just like an auto engine, the personality can be said to be uncoordinated for the tasks it must perform and out of sync.

You may not have recognized it as such, but you probably have experienced an inner awareness of your true self many times. Whenever you operate at your personal best, you catch glimpses of your true self. It's at those moments when you feel you're cooking on all four burners, when all systems are go, when you feel you can do no wrong, when you're totally in sync with yourself and the world around you.

Since most of us spend so little time functioning at our best, it is no wonder that this self of ours seems a stranger. But don't worry. We're going to change all that. By the time you've finished reading this book, you will be able to tap in to your self at will and reap the rewards that go with establishing control over your personality.

The zones are guidelines—not hard-and-fast commandments. You will have all the flexibility you want to move from one zone to the other. But these zones, which reflect a quality of territoriality much like that one observes in an animal when its domain is invaded, will assist you as nothing else can in determining successful courses of action.

Today you may be in the worst possible situation. But once you've learned to make the most of it, you will not only have achieved success for that situation, you will have laid the groundwork for future success.

Let me tell you about several clients of mine who discovered ways of putting themselves into sync—and how they benefited.

Tempers were flaring and the pressure was on everyone in the conference room to come up with a selling point for the firm's biggest customer. A hook was needed: a forceful idea that would boost their customer's lagging sales. Joanne felt good. She was concentrating, avoiding the pitfalls, and pacing herself. Her mind was working well. She easily winnowed the grain from the chaff, sorting out the good ideas from the bad. Quietly she began to assemble the pieces of the puzzle and emerge with a solution to the problem. She took her time presenting her ideas. She was in sync with herself and her situation.

It hadn't always been this way for Joanne. She used to be known around the office as someone to be wary of, a real volcano. When the pressure got too great and tempers began to flare, Joanne typically overreacted. In losing her cool, she often lost her point.

As Jack dressed to go to the party, he felt good. It was the end of summer; the weather was still hot but there was the promise of the relief that evening would bring. Jack was comfortable with himself. In less than twenty minutes he was at the party, talking, laughing, and feeling great. He was content. He was in sync.

In the past when something social was happening, Jack would feel intimidated, tongue-tied and shy. No matter that other people liked him; he never knew how to behave socially and disliked himself for his awkwardness. But Jack underwent a major change. Something wonderful had happened to him. Today he's in sync and enjoying life.

Bill was standing in the grocery line. His two-year-old son, Cody, was sitting in the basket with the remains of a peach smeared across his face. Julie, his five-year-old, was busy rearranging a cents-off candy display, and the woman behind him was moaning about how slow the checkers were. Bill felt contented and peaceful. He was in no hurry. He was in sync.

You'd never recognize Bill because he's changed so dramatically. Once upon a time, he had no time for his kids. He was too busy to do the shopping for the family. There was just enough time to study the stock market and manage his clients' portfolios.

Meredith is on the phone. Her client is in a panic about the negotiation. He wants her to get two more points on the movie contract, but the studio is balking, threatening to pull out of the entire deal. Meredith smiles and then says, "Jack, stop fretting. We're going to get another point. But just one. Insist on two and you'll blow the deal. Don't be greedy; you don't have to make it all on this picture." Meredith knew where she was in the negotiation. She was in sync.

It wasn't that long ago that Meredith was so insecure that she would not have had the courage to listen to herself. She would have tried to do what, in her heart, she knew she could not do and did not believe in.

What put Joanne, Jack, Bill, and Meredith into personal synchrony? Each got there a bit differently. Joanne got into sync because she was not taking the business anger, frustration, and anxiety personally. Jack was in sync because he was being active and outgoing. Bill was in sync because he was focused on the happiness he felt and not the slow checkers or the long lines. Meredith was in sync because she didn't assume that the upset of her clients was her fault. All these people have changed from what they were. All of them once let external events cause them anxiety and trigger inappropriate reactions. They used to look inside themselves for fault.

Now they know how to make the most of their situations. And in so doing they are in sync. They are in control.

Being in the right zone is most obvious when pressure is high and success is possible. You are in the right zone and in sync with it when everyone else steps back and you step forward or when everyone else is getting on the bandwagon and you get off or when everyone else panics and you don't. It's easy to do the right thing when there is no pressure. But when the heat is on and everyone is flailing about in confusion, that is when you need to summon your ability to achieve sync.

Stars master their circumstances. That is what makes them stars. Bottom of the ninth. Last game of the World Series. Reggie Jackson is up at bat. Crack, he hits the home run. Mary Lou Retton needs nothing less than an outstanding vault to win an Olympic gold medal. The pressure is on but as she speeds down the runway, she is in sync. She hits the springboard and vaults into space. She knows exactly what she has to do. Luciano Pavarotti at the Met. It is one of those special moments in grand opera when every voice is keyed to one magnificent swelling note, and then Pavarotti hits a piercing note—a note that seems higher, longer, and more intense than anything humanly possible. Everyone is uplifted.

Being in sync makes all the difference. It makes a difference during a championship golf match, at the breakfast table with your children, negotiating the biggest business deal of your life, and making love. It feels like the magic of being in the right place at the right time with the right stuff. It is real. You have been there many times before and may have taken it for granted. But the important thing is being able to put yourself into sync when the chips are down.

Sync is no illusion. It is not happenstance. It is an art and a skill you can learn.

Being in sync does not mean killing yourself to be in any particular place, such as Studio 54, or Yankee Stadium, or Maxim's. It means simply making the most and the best of the situation you are in.

You feel different when you're in sync. You may have thought that feeling came because you were just lucky, or because your stars were just right. But it isn't luck to be in sync. It occurs because of what you *do.*

When you are in sync you have a sense of what you can do about your life and you are willing to try it. More often than not you perceive sync only because you are out of sync so much of the time. This realization is not enough to help you. It certainly won't tell you how to achieve it. It's more important to know what is right, and how to do the right thing, than to realize that you're out of step with the world.

If you are experiencing loneliness, procrastination, anxiety, fear, relationship problems, no one has to tell you that you are out of sync. In short, you don't feel good. You aren't living up to your potential. When negative signs appear, your first reaction is to want to do something about them. This book is *not* about "doing something about what is wrong." This book is about finding out how to do something right. It is about:

Learning how to change.

Learning what it's like to be at your best.

Learning how to become your best.

Learning how to put yourself in sync.

In this book I will show you nothing less than how to live the rest of your life in sync.

Begin by thinking of life as a game. It will help you to develop the attitude you will need. By *game* I don't mean to imply that life ought to be lived frivolously or that life doesn't count. It does count. It's real and meaningful. And there are real tragedies in life. Grief and mourning and sympathy are necessary and natural human emotions. There are times when one needs to be alone, when one needs to share the feelings of disappointment and even misery that afflict one's friends and loved ones. But when carried to an extreme, they can be an unhealthy self-indulgence, a kind of destructive narcissism.

I am suggesting that even the most serious of life's challenges are better managed when one assumes what I call a "Player Attitude": when one sees the challenge as a game that can be played profitably. And one's chances of winning are improved when one understands the rules, sets one's sights on goals, and reaches out for a win.

I use the word *game* because it will help you to focus better on what you are doing and to employ a more useful, positive, compassionate attitude. It helps establish a context in which you can discover the rules for winning and discover why people lose. It will help you give your all in playing the game of life.

In a game, mistakes are O.K. and the mere playing of the game grants you a sense of accomplishment and satisfaction. Games demand positive expectations. By thinking of life as a game, you can visualize yourself as a "life athlete" with the corresponding courage and motivation and discipline. Much of your time will be spent learning how to play the game. Remember: Professional and serious amateur athletes spend 95 percent of their time preparing to play and just 5 percent actually playing. In everyday life we prepare 5 percent and play 95 percent. It's no wonder that, with so little preparation, so many of us feel overwhelmed by life's pressures and demands.

Now, in keeping with this concept of living life as a game, I'm going to ask you to consider me your personal coach. I am going to teach you how to win. I am not promising you a million dollars, a new Mercedes, or chairmanship of the board of anything. I am going to go one better. I am going to help you find your true self—to discover what you are like at your very best.

At your best you can control your life, create new options, and discover perspectives and directions never before available to you.

When you see a COACH'S TIME-OUT or a COACH'S NOTE in the book—stop for a minute and think. This is my way of chatting with you informally. They give me a way of amplifying a subject with tips and encouragement. Don't skip over them. They're important. Take your time. You can get more out of this book by reading it at a leisurely pace than by trying to get it all under your belt in a single reading.

Helping you change is the goal of this book. Nothing is harder or more rewarding than change. If you've tried to change before and failed, I'm going to ask you to try again. Take another chance. I would like you to learn how to change by taking action, and to reap the great benefits of your actions and your changes.

If you can win, you can also lose. This book will show you the high cost of failure—not failure per se, but of failure to act. Reluctance to seize the occasion lowers your success potential. Considering life a game permits you to think of your losses as temporary setbacks in the game of life. It can also keep you from thinking of yourself as a born loser.

COACH'S NOTE

Remember, you are *not* going to fail here. My job is to coach you step by step. You don't have to become perfect. Learn what you can and put what you learn to use. But don't wait for total under-

standing before trying out what you have learned. Try it right
away. Dive into the pool of life and splash around.

COACH'S TIME-OUT

Stop a moment. This isn't a magic book. It's a book about reality—a reality you're already familiar with. What it will do is help
you put what you know into action for yourself. And I'll give you
an A each time you do it.

What's Ahead

To put yourself into sync you need to develop a new attitude
about life. In the first two chapters you will find out about the
Player Attitude, the attitude of playing life as if it were a game.
The Player Attitude is rooted in knowing that *you can take action.* It is positive and accepting. It will help you adapt to changing circumstances.

Once you take steps to become a life player, you are ready to
understand the rules governing the Four Life Zones of the game
of life. The concept of these zones will help you analyze any situation. These principles are so powerful that, once you understand
them, you will never think of leaving home without them. They
permit you to read signals and achieve your goals with a mini-
mum of fuss. They keep you from making wrong turns, running
out of gas, and winding up where you don't want to be.

Each of the zones comes with a complete set of rules, regulations, and strategies for creating synchrony. When you understand the life zones you will know *where and when* it is essential
to be intimate and receptive and *where and when* you ought to
be assertive and aggressive. You will not have to focus on solving
a particular problem. Instead, you will be able to change your
perceptions in light of your own experience and know where
you are and what to do.

Following the rules governing the zones puts you into sync.
Once in sync, you are ready to learn what it is like to be "you at
your best." I will teach you not only how to be "you at your
best" but how to transform this condition into an active

awareness. This awareness will be the psychological gyroscope that keeps you steady, on your feet, and in control.

If you know in which of the Four Life Zones you find yourself and you possess a reference point of "you at your best," then you will have changed your outlook on life. It is just this fresh outlook that great athletes experience, great scientists draw upon, and great musicians feel. It gives them a special feel for what they are doing. They actually see things differently from the way most people do.

While depth of perception may seem second nature to a person of genius, it is also a quality you can cultivate. Changing your view almost magically opens up opportunities for change and an escape from dreary, binding circumstances.

The final chapters teach you how it feels to change, what comes first and what comes next and so forth. Taking these steps spells the difference between being an amateur and a professional, and between being a professional and a champion. Take them one step at a time, as they come. You don't want to expect too much of yourself at the start of this learning process.

You can put yourself into sync. The big question, of course, is how?

Getting Your Act Together

All the new information you'll be receiving in this book may be processed more easily if you keep in mind four important questions. They will enable you to understand the dynamics of almost any situation you happen to be in. But it is your Player Attitude that will push you to take that first step of *using* the four questions as a checklist for success.

QUESTION ONE: Where are you right now?
QUESTION TWO: What are your needs?
QUESTION THREE: What images are you using?
QUESTION FOUR: What signals are you sending and what signals are you receiving?

QUESTION ONE: Where are you right now? To answer this you will have to know about the *zones* described in Chapters

Three to Eight. The four zones determine what kind of actions need to be taken if you want to be successful in whatever you are doing.

QUESTION TWO: What are your needs? By the time we are finished with this book you are going to be an expert on human needs—your own and the needs of other people. When you know what you need and how to fill your needs, you will find yourself "at your best." Merely having and recognizing needs (not even fulfilling those needs) nourishes the personality. And a multiplicity of needs nourishes you more than just a few.

If you don't know what you want, your chances of happiness are minimal. In Chapters Twelve to Fifteen I will take you through many different kinds of needs and ways of meeting those needs. Once you know what you need, how do you go about getting satisfaction? The answer is explained in Chapters Sixteen, Seventeen, and Eighteen.

QUESTION THREE: What images are you using? Images are the roles you assume in interacting with the world. An image is functional when it fills your needs and it is nonfunctional when it doesn't. If being a "good girl" or "good boy" (i.e., doing just as you are told) once filled your need for family attention, it was functional. But if as an adult you continue your image as Goody-Two-Shoes with your boss, you will probably find it less than a winner.

Images are like clothes: They become worn out, threadbare, and out-of-date. We outgrow them. But because we have created them, we can change them. We are not stuck with them forever. We can design our own fashions and we can control our images.

QUESTION FOUR: Which signals are you sending and which ones are you receiving? We will answer this question in Chapters Nineteen and Twenty. Airplanes are guided by radar; bats, by a form of sonar; and humans, by a multitude of signals. Human signals are as clear and distinct as traffic lights. When you know how to read and send appropriate signals you dramatically increase your ability to put yourself into sync.

Answering these four questions will be simple by the time you finish this book. As an added bonus you will also have discovered some new options in every aspect of your life, making it easier to act and to change.

* * *

Remember, your success will depend on taking new action, no matter how small that action is. So very often, people want new results without having to bother to change their modus operandi. They want their engine to hum along at top speed without ever giving it a tune-up. Or they want to try out something new without changing their perspective. Benefits wrought by half measures are almost always of brief duration.

People look for quick answers because change has always struck them as difficult if not futile. Many people will try almost anything once, as long as they don't have to invest too much time or energy. They say to themselves, "If it works, fine; if not, nothing lost."

But when you steer clear of risk, something *has* been lost. Some hope has been lost. Some motivation, too. You can lose your will to excel. I want to teach you how to make long-term changes by building up your hope and stirring you to excellence. I am going to give you a recipe that, when followed diligently, will assure positive results.

How many times have you attributed failure to circumstances or to some ornery and incorrigible quality within you? Well, you won't have to do that anymore. Success comes from personal synchrony, which you can acquire for yourself by using this book. Are you ready to get started? Let's go to Chapter One and find out how to sharpen your Player Attitude.

Section One

SUCCESS
STARTS WITH
ATTITUDE

CHAPTER

·1·

Success Starts with Attitude

A *ttitude is where change and success begin.* Attitude is the filter through which you view life. It is the melody behind the words. It is your basic rhythm. And you can develop and shape your attitude.

Your present attitude may not be serving you well. It may not be as effective as it might be. Now it will become possible for you to acquire a brand-new attitude, one that will carry you through the rest of your life in a positive and exciting way.

I call this new attitude the Player Attitude. Player as in Athlete. Life-athlete. *When you have the Player Attitude you are playing life as though it were a game.* And that means you are ready for action. My clinical experience has shown me that when people take action, they increase their good feelings and decrease their depression. It is through action that they connect to life and get themselves moving in directions that give them the rewards that make life worth living. The Player Attitude has enthusiasm and energy. It makes the most of whatever you are doing. It doesn't mean you always like what you have to do. *It simply means that you know success starts from doing the best with whatever you're involved with right now.* The Player Attitude is what winners in all the different arenas of life use to get them through the tough times and to propel them toward their goals.

Get your mind off your problem and concentrate instead on the rewards you'll get from adopting a Player Attitude. Then strive for those rewards. The Player Attitude gives you immediate good feelings, which in turn help you solve problems with joy and a motivation to continue your success pattern.

COACH'S NOTE

Throughout this book I will give you tests and checklists. They are teaching devices. You can't fail any of them. Everything in this book is designed to help you change and feel good. Including the tests.

You will need reasons to change, and these reasons will stem from your attitude. When this attitude becomes second nature to you, you'll find yourself in sync without even trying.

First, let's look at your current attitude. Here is an attitude checklist I use with my clients.

Attitude Checklist

Just check the statement, A or B, that you feel more accurately describes your attitude. Put down your first impulse. Remember, no one is going to read it but you. Once you finish this test, we will discuss it.

1. A) You get pleasure from the risk of taking new action _____
   B) You feel more comfortable observing rather than participating _____

2. A) You challenge your old attitudes _____
   B) You are confident that your perceptions are almost always bang on target _____

3. A) You approach work and success with your goals in mind _____
   B) You tend to be distracted from your goals by problems or other people _____

4. A) You are actively involved in improving your relationships _____

B) Your relationships seem fixed almost from the start and follow an unchanging quality: If they are good, terrific. If not, then, tough _____

5. A) In any situation you do your best _____
   B) You put yourself out only when you feel it's really important _____

6. A) You treat yourself and others with care and respect _____
   B) You can get pretty down on yourself and others _____

7. A) You appreciate others for themselves _____
   B) You find yourself judging others, especially when things are not going the way you want _____

8. A) You realize that you can change how you feel and think _____
   B) You feel stuck with the feelings and thoughts you have _____

9. A) You consistently feel that you're doing your best _____
   B) You spend a lot of time feeling out of sorts with yourself and the world _____

10. A) You train yourself to improve performance _____
    B) You believe your personality is pretty much set when you're young _____

11. A) You know how to read people and situations _____
    B) Other people and situations are a mystery to you _____

12. A) You reward yourself for what you do well _____
    B) You expect yourself to do well without reward _____

13. A) You reward others for what they do well _____
    B) You don't want to spoil others with rewards, or you feel sure that they know that you appreciate them _____

14. A) You are consciously working toward becoming aware of how your life works and why_____
 B) Life works in mysterious, immutable ways_____

15. A) Once you see yourself making the same mistake again, you try to correct it_____
 B) You keep making the same mistakes_____

16. A) You wake up eager to get out of bed and get going_____
 B) You wonder where you are going to find the motivation to get through the day_____

17. A) You enjoy taking part in almost any situation_____
 B) You tend to be an observer_____

18. A) You realize that things often go wrong with no one at fault or out to "get you"_____
 B) You can't seem to change, but many situations make you feel guilty or anxious_____

If you had eighteen As and no Bs, you have the Player Attitude Potential.

What we need to do now is take this Player Attitude and put it into action. Your biggest problem is not to get trapped by all the Nonplayer Attitudes around you.

If you had more As than Bs, you have the Player Attitude.

You obviously have begun to see the light at the end of the tunnel, but you may be having a hard time getting there. Don't despair. I have found that people with Player Attitude potential often just need some coaching to win in life. Many people who score more As than Bs start off with good intentions and then become negative when they fail. If this sounds like you, you are in good shape. We will help you look out for the stumbling blocks along the path to success.

If you had more Bs than As, *you have a "Nonplayer Attitude"*.

A Nonplayer Attitude is negative, judgmental, and passive. Don't feel bad. You have the most to gain from developing the Player Attitude of playing life like a game. If you are in this category, notice how your Nonplayer Attitude is trying to put you down right now. You can challenge and change your attitude, and feel great as soon as you do.

Is Your Attitude Keeping You from Success?

Nothing is more painful to me than to see people with great potential who are unaware that their attitude—and only their attitude—is keeping them from success.

To become all that you can be, you have to break the attitude barrier. By merely reaching for your potential, you will feel a contentment, an understanding, a good feeling, and a peace in your life that you may have felt before only on rare occasions.

Change is a must. It is a difficult but not impossible task. I know because all my work has been devoted to exploring new methods for behavioral, psychological, physiological, social, emotional, intellectual, and spiritual change. I know about change because of the changes I have made and the changes I have helped others make.

The main risk of change is the possibility of failure. On occasion I have changed because I wanted something more. At other times I have changed because I felt so terrible the way I was. In either case, change did not come without pain. This book is a synopsis of the years of human change I have witnessed. It involves the lives of thousands of people and many thinkers. It offers you some simple, direct, and effective methods of change. It required me, in the writing of it, to make major changes in my life-style, outlook, and behavior.

Even Psychologists Get the Blues

My changes did not come easily. Many of them were provoked by great pain and grief. In November 1980, for instance, I lived through a major professional crisis.

For a decade I had worked closely with a group of psychologists. We had established clinics in Los Angeles, Boston, Munich, Hawaii, San Francisco, and Montreal. We enjoyed a string of professional successes. We earned a good living. We seemed to be the fondest of friends as well as a close-knit team of therapists.

But when our mettle was tested by stress, we broke. Our

friendship turned into the bitterest enmity. We had failed to work on our attitudes toward each other and our work. In falling out among ourselves, we demolished what we had so pains-takingly constructed.

The most painful part for me was the realization that our friendships had been so thin. Virtually overnight, men and women to whom I would have entrusted my life were gone from my life.

I felt utterly abandoned and lost. I did not know where to turn. I became depressed. I was so distraught that almost anything from an old ballad to the TV nightly news would make me cry. When I was at my most depressed, I saw no way out of my plight. Nothing I had done or achieved before mattered. My spirit was crushed.

One day while I watched two boys playing in a park, a vivid childhood memory came back to haunt me. I remembered sitting in a classroom at my grade school in Phoenix. It was one of those times in each school day when the only thing I cared about was going home to play. I couldn't concentrate for one more minute on what Sister Prudentia was saying. The numbers in my mathe-matics book would bubble up on the page and transform them-selves into Sanskrit, and my body would just ache with an eagerness to get out and play.

When I got home I would get into my play clothes and my play shoes and then run outside. I had to play. It was more than just *wanting* to play. I simply *had* to. I would run across the street to Harry's house and yell up for him to come out. We would play football, baseball, war, cards, airplanes, kites, skating . . . anything. The *particular game* didn't matter. It was life that we were play-ing, and it was playing itself that would revitalize us for the next day of school.

There were even times at school when learning was just like play. Those were the times when the excitement of the learn-ing—not the fear of the test—would sweep us all up into the game of knowledge. But that was the rare case. It took a while but the teachers finally reached me. I learned to take my work seriously. When I moved to Los Angeles, school became a profes-sion. It was no longer a game. And I lost the feeling of playing that I used to have.

Those two boys playing triggered the discovery of something I had left behind in my childhood. But it was something, fortunately, that was still deep within me.

I discovered I had given up the *attitude* of play. My colleagues and I had created our own crisis because we had become too serious, too important, too focused on work, and we weren't paying enough attention to the other arenas of our lives. As a kid, I would dare anything. I was always eager and willing. I was obsessed with the joy of doing.

As I reviewed my life, I realized that I learned about life, about feeling good, and about other people, more through play than anything else. In play there was breath, and sweat, and a special connection to life, a bond to other people, and an intimacy with myself. *Playing consists of two things: the playing itself and a positive outlook.*

A child plays with concentration, attention, and endless motivation. These are precisely the qualities adults long to possess. When we take *ourselves* more seriously than *what* we are doing, we have lost the enjoyment of life and what we are doing becomes work. And work without the attitude of play becomes drudgery, a chore we want to be over and done with. The problem is that as adults we will spend the greatest part of our lives working. But instead of having an attitude of play, we drag ourselves through the day, trying to get done what we have to do, get it over and done with. The process of work takes a backseat to the final outcome. We are waiting to get done before we feel good. Done with what? This moment is our life. Life doesn't begin on Friday afternoon or with our vacation. *This* is it. Here, now. The stakes are terrific.

Think about a child. *A child is living life and playing at the same time.* You had that ability at one time and you can have it again because it is still within you. In play the end result is important but no more important than the doing. Playing is the moment-to-moment experience of "you at your best." You can transform your attitudes so that you bring to your adult life the same good feeling you had when you played as a child.

What Is a Player Attitude?

The Player Attitude is that of a life-athlete playing, participating, giving his or her all. It is a positive, energetic, and assertive attitude. When you have a Player Attitude you are willing to let go of your old beliefs. You give yourself the training and care you need to enhance your self-esteem. You trust that you will come out ahead.

COACH'S TIME-OUT: "Let's talk."

Sometimes it is easier to understand something about yourself by seeing it in other people. Think about someone you know who has a Nonplayer Attitude. A Nonplayer Attitude is negative, judgmental, and passive. A person with a Nonplayer Attitude is waiting for someone else or something outside to provide the feeling that comes from being "you at your best." If you have a Nonplayer Attitude, you view your beliefs as facts, your perceptions as the only truth, and your thoughts as the ultimate reality.

Now think about it. What is it like to be with the person who has a Nonplayer Attitude? Now think about someone you know who has a Player Attitude. Remember, the Player Attitude means doing the best you can anywhere. It is playing life as a game. What is it like to be with a Player Attitude person? Now take a closer look at your attitude in different situations. Remember, you can have a Player Attitude in some parts of your life and not in others.

COACH'S EXERCISE: "Let's take some action."

Let's compare the two attitudes side by side and see the differences. Just put a check next to the qualities you notice in yourself.

Player Attitude	*Nonplayer Attitude*
_____ You reinforce the positive	_____ You stress the negative
_____ You point out what is wrong in a constructive way	_____ You point out what is wrong in a critical and negative way
_____ You are nonjudgmental but observant	_____ You are accusing, blaming, blinded by your own point of view
_____ You fully participate	_____ You passively participate
_____ You avoid negative criticism	_____ You give negative criticism
_____ You give positive suggestions	_____ You withhold positive evaluations
_____ You play life like a game	_____ You endure life
_____ You work up to your full potential	_____ You get by and procrastinate
_____ You have an inner reference	_____ You are controlled by outer events
_____ You are compassionate	_____ You seek punishment, revenge
_____ You make the most of the situation	_____ You think this is the way it has to be
_____ You play moment to moment	_____ It's always "do or die"
_____ You use strategy, prepare, scout	_____ You hope for the best
_____ You do what you can now	_____ You'll do it when you feel good
_____ You think mistakes are permissible	_____ You regard mistakes as wrong
_____ You use mistakes as cues	_____ You think mistakes are judgments
_____ You know this is only your opinion	_____ You think your viewpoint is the truth
_____ You are a teammate	_____ You see yourself as the star

Player Attitude	*Nonplayer Attitude*
_____ You do what you can in each situation	_____ You think the world or someone owes you something
_____ You understand others' weaknesses and limitations	_____ You criticize others for their weaknesses and limitations

Have you checked more As than Bs? Use that information to take the next action.

Now list the kind of attitude (Player or Nonplayer) you have in the following areas of your life:

Work_____
Play_____
Sex_____
Family_____
Friends_____
Spouse or Lover_____

1. What did you notice?

2. Do you have a Player Attitude in some parts of your life and not in others?

3. Think about it. Is the Player Attitude in one area of your life canceled out by your Nonplayer Attitude in others?

4. In what area of life do you have the most trouble? What kind of attitude do you have in that area?

What You Can Expect

If you want your Player Attitude to come alive in your life, then you must start expecting it from others.

Relationships. The Player Attitude makes you realize that you may have differences of opinion, and even disputes, but you need not treat each other as though you're on the opposing team. The Player Attitude in a relationship helps you both assume the responsibility for doing the best you can. No one plays the mother or the child. You don't accuse, attack, or try to control.

Family. Parents have the hardest time deciding how much they can demand from their children. Your children may be very different from you, but they are your children and you are in the same family. You can demand and expect a Player Attitude.

Work. Player Attitudes at work would revolutionize the workplace. If you are the boss, strive to teach your employees and subordinates about the Player Attitude. When everyone feels that he or she is on the same team, productivity soars.

Friends. Friendship without a Player Attitude never quite takes off. By itself, the Player Attitude can help launch a real friendship.

Whatever you're involved with: family, relationships, work—you have to fight for a true Player Attitude. The adoption of a Nonplayer Attitude allows you to be controlled and almost guarantees failure. Stand up for what feels best to you.

How Do You Create a Player Attitude?

By answering the questions I have already asked you, you have begun to tell me your life story. If you are like most of my clients, at this point you may want to rush headlong to do something more, something dramatic.

Stop. Don't do a thing. I believe in a very gentle and slow approach to change. Master each step. Right now the fastest way for you to change is to focus on other people's attitudes. Notice if they are using Player Attitudes or Nonplayer Attitudes. This will help you sharpen your Player Attitude because you will no longer be oblivious to what is happening around you. Where you used to feel vaguely uneasy, you will understand that the unease is created by someone's Nonplayer Attitude. Before long you will automatically notice your own attitude. Once you start noticing your own attitude, it becomes possible to change it. Don't worry if you think this exercise is not hard enough. Lasting change, in my experience, takes place by a succession of small, positive steps. Try to master each step as it comes. Before long the steps will add up to a major change—and you will be surprised with the results.

COACH'S TIME-OUT

Try for a moment to recall that childhood feeling of playing. Remember what it was like playing with some special friend. Think about your total absorption by the game and the utter joy you felt. I want you to use that feeling as your reference for developing your Player Attitude. Take a minute right now to remember that special time.

1. How old were you?
2. Where did the experience take place?
3. How did you feel?
4. What happened to that feeling?

In my practice I try to get my clients to recall the best parts of themselves, parts that they may have forgotten. Then I get them to use their best as their *model* for a new adult attitude or behavior. I want you to change according to your own standards, standards that you have within yourself. That way you won't get lost trying to be what you imagine you should be or what someone else wants you to be.

Review

I have given you a certain amount of information. Before you go on to the next chapter I want you to master this chapter. Review it. Play with it. Remember, you can have the right information, the right idea, but if you have the wrong attitude, *you* are decreasing your chances for success. Your attitude is the extra factor working for your success.

The Player Attitude will be very important to your new success. You have the Player Attitude when you play life like a game and you bring gusto and commitment to *whatever* you are doing. So many people think that if they worry about what will happen, it somehow makes what they are doing more real and important. It doesn't! In fact, worry decreases the sum of what you get from any experience—the joy of doing it. No matter how many things are going on in your life, all you can do right now is what is possible at this very moment. Take control over your attitude. Remember, it is your attitude and you can damn well have the attitude you choose. Having a Player Attitude doesn't mean you always like what you are doing or the one you're dealing with, but it does mean you give every venture your all, and when you are finished, *then* you make the changes you want. Otherwise, you become a victim of circumstance and act accordingly. With the attitude of playing life like a game, you know you cannot control what happens, but you can control what you do and how you feel—and you can do your best.

But how do you develop this Player Attitude? Let me demonstrate by telling you about Shelly, a former client of mine. If you are ready, let's go on to Chapter Two.

·2·

How to Develop a Player Attitude

I explore with my clients the changes I see them making. Then the entire group discusses these changes. So very often, when you run into difficulty trying to make a change, you think there is something wrong with you. Change requires you to attempt new behaviors that you don't possess. Almost inevitably, this means that you are going to experience failure. Let me coach you in developing a Player Attitude by telling you about a client who went from having a full-fledged Nonplayer Attitude to a Player attitude. Her name is Shelly.

SHELLY
Age: 38
Marital Status: Married (first marriage—16 years to Randy)
Children: Two (Matthew, 14, and Karen, 10)
Occupation: Accounting firm executive

When Shelly walked into my New York office, she was wearing a brown-tweed designer suit and she looked impeccable. She very assertively introduced herself and then sat silently. I looked at her closely. Her jaw was set in a clenched bite and she slowly and unconsciously ground her teeth. Her breathing was shallow from the upper chest. Shelly was having a hard time catching her breath. It was as if she were wearing a steel girdle. Her nails were polished, but her hands twitched, flitting from her lap to her sides and then back to her lap. She was fifteen pounds overweight and her suit showed the bulges. She was a middle-level accounting executive caught between the entrenched upper-level male executives and the fresh-from-college MBAs.

Shelly had been in the middle of her MBA graduating class and was a kind of pioneer in what had been a male bastion. For the past ten years she had been preoccupied with the conflict between her family's demands and the stresses of her career. She had married soon after college and had had two children before going on to graduate school. She had fought her way up the executive ladder and then, five years ago, seemed to get stuck. She was starting to buckle under the pressures of job and family. What Shelly told me during the course of our first four visits is condensed in what follows.

"I don't know what is wrong, but I am just about to give up. I find myself screaming at my children for the littlest things and my husband and I fight whenever we are in the same room. When I get up in the morning I am in a hurry. I start breakfast and then wake up the kids. By that time Randy, my husband, is showering, and if everything goes perfectly, by the time he gets done with his shower the kids will be ready to eat. And then I might shower while he serves them breakfast. But that never happens.

"Sometimes I walk out into the kitchen and discover I am out of milk or coffee or eggs. Or I'll start the bacon and go get the kids up and one or another of them will be moving in extra-slow motion. At other times I will think everything is going fine while I am showering, but when I get out of the shower I discover no one has eaten breakfast. I start off my day tense.

"At work the pressure is unbelievable. I go from meeting to meeting. Or I'm on the phone with three calls waiting. There is always the conflict between being assertive and being put down for being a woman. By the time I get home, I feel exhausted, but as soon as I get there I have to start thinking about dinner and the kids.

"I feel so guilty about the kids. I just don't have the time for them and what they need. They are both good students, but Karen, the younger, is having trouble with school. I find myself snapping at them more and more and finding fault with them for everything they do. I want them to keep their rooms clean and to help out around the house and they fight me.

"Randy and I should probably get a divorce. We haven't been close, really close, in years. I keep picking fights with him; I can't stop criticizing and correcting him.

"The other day I got home and Matthew was watching television, and I started to yell at him because it was too loud and he didn't have his homework started. I kept yelling until he burst into tears and ran into his room. I didn't know what to do. So I just poured myself a drink. By the time Randy got home I was feeling terribly guilty. I told him what had happened and instead of being understanding toward me, he was punishing. He didn't give me any support or sympathy. He told me if I was better organized, then I could handle it. The next thing I knew I had launched into a major shouting match. I *watched* myself do the whole thing. I can't even believe what I did."

What did I know about Shelly? I knew a lot. First of all, she and her husband were in a negative cycle. They were headed for divorce because the *needs* of neither one were being met. Instead of communicating and meeting each other's needs, they were indulging their emotions by casting blame, accusations, and criticism. Randy didn't know how to support Shelly, and she didn't know how to ask for support. Her children were entering their teens. The potential for disaster was tremendous.

But the clearest thing I heard as Shelly talked was her Nonplayer Attitude. She *talked* like a victim. She was negative, hostile, and anxious. She didn't expect things to change, and she spent more time feeling guilty than trying to make the most of situations. She had quit on herself and her life. There was no play, no game, no fun, no joy in her life. Shelly had lost what many adults lose—the *attitude* of playing. Shelly approached life with the notion that she had to be perfect, and when she wasn't, she thought that something was wrong with her or someone else. Her attitude drove her to think that if she could just fix the problems of the screaming, the yelling, and the criticizing, everything would be all right. The focus on problems is a major characteristic of a Nonplayer Attitude. Shelly was right in realizing that she had to do something, but she was headed in the wrong direction. Her first step toward success came with a change in attitude.

Let's quickly review the two attitudes. We have displayed them on pages 39–40. If you think about what Shelly was saying and how she was saying it, you will perceive her attitude.

To help Shelly start developing a Player Attitude, I got her to talk about the rewards she wanted in her life. I knew if I could help her develop a Player Attitude, we could get her into sync. I asked Shelly to talk to me about what she wanted, what would make her feel good, and what would do something for her. She, on the other hand, kept trying to get me to focus on her problems. She was not easily persuaded to talk about rewards and what she really needed. She thought what I wanted her to talk about wouldn't lead anywhere; she thought the way to solve the problem was to attack it and solve it. It took time for her to learn that there was a far better method.

Many times you have felt down, helpless, depressed, and giving up, but your attitude is something you can control. You just have to make a decision. Since you can do only one thing at any one moment, get your Player Attitude started; you just have to decide to take some action. It could be talking to a friend, working out at the gym, cleaning your house, returning a phone call, or smiling at a stranger.

I know that when you are feeling bad it seems easier to identify a problem and try to solve it than to start talking about what you need, but that is *not* how to get into sync. The way to the right place is to develop a Player Attitude. It might seem a little out of the way at first, but I want to coach you so that you can remain in sync, once you're there. The steps to synchrony might seem too small and too slow for you but you have to take your time to build a foundation you can use the rest of your life.

COACH'S TIME OUT

If you develop the attitude of playing life like a game, you will begin to see the rules of the life game—because all games have rules. Without rules there would be no play, no winning, no good time. One of the most important rules of success is to play life like a game. This first step in developing a Player Attitude is a big one, because:

1. If the life game is played by rules, then you can understand how to win.
2. If life is a game, then you can improve your skills and you aren't stuck with the way you are playing right now.

Shelly had tried to inject a kind of synchrony into her life and it hadn't worked. She sought change by working on her problems. But solving a problem wasn't a big enough reward to induce long-term change. Harvard psychologist Chris Argyris and his MIT colleague Donald Schon have said that only 5 percent of people are able to change because change is dependent on knowing how change will be rewarded. And like Shelly, most people don't even think in terms of rewards. And although they want to change, they are missing this key ingredient, and get stuck.

Needs: The Key to Developing a Player Attitude

Your entire psychology and physiology is a need-satisfying machine. If you don't know what you need, you have no direction. Knowing what you and others need turns your human machine on, and once your human machine gets moving, it gives you a sense of competence and security. The Player Attitude comes directly from responding to your needs. Reaching for your potential means you have turned your machine on and you are fueling it with your needs. You don't even have to know exactly how to satisfy a perceived need immediately. *Just knowing about your needs* helps you get started toward personal synchrony.

Having direction is another of the key factors in successful change. Knowing what you need is not a sign of selfishness or self-absorption but a sign of self-esteem. Most people don't know what they need and don't take the time to find out until they are desperate. At the last moment they settle for what is available. Clearly, Shelly didn't begin to know what she needed. It was no wonder she had a Nonplayer Attitude.

When the air is filled with blaming and irrational anger, you know there's a Nonplayer present. The Player posture readies you for rewards and allows you to see problems as stepping-stones to the goal. This Player Attitude gets you into a perspective where you can learn, where you can do something new, and where you can win.

A Player's needs are, in many respects, a kind of reward. Mere recognition of who you are and what you want can be challenging and exhilarating. People who don't know what they need search from person to person, situation to situation, hoping that what they need will drop on their doorstep as a gift from heaven. And then time and again they wind up disappointed and frustrated. Shelly had the secret hope that solving one more problem would give her what she needed.

Problems can be seductive. The solution to the next problem seems to offer just what you wanted, but solutions bring only temporary relief. There is always a new problem.

Time and again Shelly would sit down with Randy to solve a problem. They both believed that it was their "lack of communication" or "not enough time together" that caused their unhappiness. No matter how much they talked, the relationship failed to improve. What was missing was a change of attitude. When Shelly became a Player, she learned how to satisfy both her husband and herself.

COACH'S EXERCISE

Think about the possibility for success in a relationship, at work, and in the family, with the following kinds of attitudes. Then rate each question 1–10, with 10 being the highest possible rating for success.

Work

You and your colleague both have a Nonplayer Attitude. Rate your chances for success _____

Your attitude is Player and your colleague's attitude is Nonplayer. Rate your chances for success _____

Your attitude is Nonplayer and your colleague's attitude is Player. Rate your chances for success _____

You and your colleague both have a Player Attitude. Rate your chances for success _____

Family
You and your family all have Nonplayer Attitudes. Rate your
   chances for success _____
Your attitude is Player and your family's attitude is Nonplayer.
   Rate your chances for success _____
Your attitude is Nonplayer and your family's attitude is Player.
   Rate your chances for success _____
You and your family all have Player Attitudes. Rate your chances
   for success _____

Relationship
You and your mate both have a Nonplayer Attitude. Rate your
   chances for success _____
Your attitude is Player and your mate's attitude is Nonplayer.
   Rate your chances for success _____
Your attitude is Nonplayer and your mate's attitude is Player.
   Rate your chances for success _____
You and your mate both have a Player Attitude. Rate your
   chances for success _____

This exercise teaches you some important things. Life is tough
enough, but when a Nonplayer is pitted against a Nonplayer it
becomes intolerable. Before you beat your head against a wall in
frustration, examine and work on your attitude. Don't wait for
someone else to change before you do. And don't wait for someone else to understand you. You can't even guess what another
person is thinking until you adopt a Player Attitude.

Many other clients are trapped by their attitudes. Let's take a
look.

TONY
Age: 32
Marital Status: Married (4 years to Sheila)
Children: None
Occupation: Art Director

Tony first came to see me because he wanted to become more
effective at work. He was a warm and very charming man. He had
an easy way of talking but was having a hard time getting ahead.
His goal was career success. As we developed strategies for his

success, I kept pointing out to him how his Nonplayer Attitude was becoming transparent. Tony attempted new Player approaches at work, but then his old Nonplayer ways overcame and depressed him.

"This won't work anyway," he would say. "This is too much effort." Tony was oblivious to his attitude and how it was affecting him. Finally it all became clear.

One afternoon after work, as he sat on a bench in Grand Central Station, waiting for the Stratford 6:15 commuter train, he finally realized that he, indeed, had a Nonplayer Attitude. It was a train delay announcement. He called me that night and said, "I heard it, my Nonplayer Attitude. I couldn't believe it when I heard it. I didn't know that the train would be late. But a little voice inside me told me that normally this minor frustration would have put me into a rotten frame of mind. By the time I got home, I would have been furious. But instead I realized that I did not have to let one late train get the better of me. Trains are late all the time. What was I fuming about? Why was I losing control? I did not have to let a trifle like that get the better of me." Tony had exposed his Nonplayer Attitude. In the sessions that followed, he learned how great a gap existed between the attitude he had grown up with and the attitudes that he was capable of adopting. He knew he could do it all differently.

JUDITH
Age: 24
Marital Status: Single
Occupation: Advertising Account Executive Assistant

Judith first decided to seek help because she had been told by her internist that she was depressed, which she did not like to hear. Judith is a very pretty dark-haired woman with a slight frame. She often had a frown on her face but every so often she would smile. And that smile could warm the heart of Ebenezer Scrooge. Her conversation betrayed an attitude that viewed everything as a problem to be resolved. She struck me as a younger version of Shelly. Judith found and resolved problems in every part of her life.

Except her biggest problem: She was still unhappy. Her problem-solving attitude was so strong that she was never able to keep her focus on her goals and successes. Problems with her parents, with her boyfriends, with her bosses, all diverted her from what she wanted to do. I kept pointing out to her that she had all the tools she needed to be successful, that it was her negative and problem-solving obsession that kept her from success.

Judith wanted me to get involved in helping her solve problems. I refused. I was going to stick to helping her change her attitude. I knew if she could change her attitude, then she would focus on her needs, and her own problems would be solved as a by-product. Judith's breakthrough came while she was talking to her mother on the phone one afternoon. She finally heard in her mother's constant complaining the very syndrome I told her that she had. Her mother was negative about everything from the weather to the condition of the vegetables in the grocery store. Judith understood what it meant to have a Nonplayer Attitude— it meant being just like her mother—unhappy. It was the start of Judith's development of her Player Attitude. The great weight of depression began to lift from her.

The change in attitude is only the first step. It's not the whole answer. When your attitude change is real, it sets the stage for your new behavior.

Judith and Tony and Shelly were having problems in their lives just like the rest of us. It is important to know that your problems are not really "yours"—they are just problems. One person has a problem with weight, another with sex, another with shyness. Problems aren't bad in themselves. Problems don't mean you are sick or that there is something wrong with you. Problems are just challenges and cues. When you recognize a problem, it means you have an opportunity to change. Remember, if you didn't have some notion that things could be better, you wouldn't think you had a problem.

Solving problems isn't a guarantee of success. You start with attitude. If you put yourself into life as an athlete and you are willing to play the game, then you can change. Your problems simply inform you that you require change in your life.

As a coach, I first want to identify a player's attitude. Does this person want to do something to improve performance? *Attitude is where success begins.* Successful employers look for the "right attitude" when interviewing job applicants. Personnel directors consider a positive attitude one of the most valuable assets an applicant has to offer. Consider the difference between going to the doctor's office because there is something wrong with you and consulting a coach to help you play better. Usually when you walk into a doctor's office, you feel like a victim. When you walk onto the playing field, you want to act, to participate, and to win.

COACH'S EXERCISE

Let's take another look at your attitude. In order to further your attitude change you must need to become *aware* of the attitude you are carrying around. Watch how people react to you. Do you have an attitude that is getting in your way, perhaps one you are unaware of? What is similar in the way different people react to you? If you notice that you have a Nonplayer Attitude, give it up. Switch to the Player Attitude and go on. If you need reminding as to what that entails go back to the attitude checklist on pages 39–40. Remember, we aren't in a hurry.

Your Player Attitude is a powerful inner tool that is vital to your health, happiness, and success. In a study by Langer and Rodin it was reported that people who felt they had some control over their environment fared better than those who felt no responsibility. A research report sponsored by the California Department of Mental Health stated, "Heredity is estimated to contribute about 20% to our health status, environment about 25%, and approximately 50% is related to *lifestyle.*" The implication is that you can take control over your own life-style and gain that 50 percent edge in your health and happiness. The same report showed that people who resisted stress most effectively shared a "specific set of attitudes about life . . .: *an openness to change, a feeling of involvement in their daily lives, and a sense of control over life and the events they experience.*"

When you have adopted a Player Attitude, you have begun to acquire the power to make your life your own. Shelly had begun. (Don't forget about Shelly, because we will follow her progress throughout the book.) It became possible to teach her how to begin living in sync once she perceived the nature of her attitude.

How Do You Develop This New Attitude?

Does it seem that it might be too hard to do? Have you tried and failed? When I first started coaching people in developing the Player Attitude, they often thought it would be impossible. They would ask, "How do you know that if I make the effort to develop a new attitude it isn't just self-deception?"

I have worked for years developing my own Player Attitude and I still refer back time and again to the checklist to find out if my Nonplayer Attitude has resurfaced. When I am feeling my worst it is because I have stopped taking action and feel helpless. I have found that I don't have to live that way. If you take action, you won't either.

COACH'S NOTE

You might want to take a break here. Think about what you have learned so far. Do you feel comfortable with what you have learned or do you need to sleep on it? Would you perhaps like to go back over it and read it again? It took me years to understand just what was written in this chapter. Take your time reading this book. Remember: We're trying to help you change a lifetime of habit. There is no rush! Proceed at your pace.

If you are ready to go ahead now, let's go on to Chapter Three and find out more about personal synchrony.

Section Two

THE
RIGHT
PLACE

·3·

The Right Zone
Learning Test

There is a right place. But it isn't where most people are looking.

Sally and Tom thought the right place was Chicago and his new job. Then the right place became their new apartment. Then the right place became the new house with the new baby. For Sally and Tom the right place was always the next place. It always seemed that where they were was never a solid right place.

Michael thought the right place was getting into the best college, but it changed to the dean's list, and then to law school, and then to his first big job.

Bobbie thought the right place would be in her next relationship. She was always starting over and getting over what she had started. It was the same for Bobbie as for Michael and Sally and Tom: The right place was always just ahead and never behind.

Sound familiar? How many people can you name who are the same way? Are you that way?

The right place exists. You are in the right place when you are making the most of the situation you are in. That sounds easy, but the reality of doing it is something entirely different. To help you make the most of the situation you are in, I want to teach you about the Four Life Zones. When you know about them, you will know how to be more effective at your job, with your spouse or lover, and with family and friends. It will make you a tougher life-competitor and a more caring human being.

The Right Place

Knowing what zone you are in helps you make the most of the situation you are in and the results are nothing less than spectacular. Think about it. Each time you are interacting with another person wherever you are, you are in one of four different life zones. The zones go from the outermost zone (Public), to the next and most frequently used zone (Social), and then to the two innermost zones (Personal and Intimate).

The outermost zone is the PUBLIC ZONE. Access to the Public Zone is open to anyone. For example, you are in the Public Zone when you are walking around the city streets window-shopping. In the Public Zone you find information, stimulation. The next zone in the circle is the SOCIAL ZONE. You are in the Social Zone whenever you are engaged in an activity. The Social Zone is an activity zone in which you participate. When you go to work or the gym you are in the Social Zone, because you are there to perform an activity.

The third circle is the PERSONAL ZONE. You are in the Personal Zone when you are sharing what you feel about yourself. You feel vulnerable in the Personal Zone because you are revealing your innermost thoughts and feelings. In the Personal Zone there is a sharing. You are not looking for a resolution; it is an experiencing zone. For example, you are in the Personal Zone when you sit down with a friend and you talk about yourself and you get that warm but shaky feeling in your stomach. And finally, the innermost zone is the INTIMATE ZONE. You are in the Intimate Zone when you care about, love, and connect with another person. In the Intimate Zone you are concerned with how what you do affects someone else. And you accept others and yourself as you are. It is intimate if you can really love another person and he or she loves you.

Here is a quick look at some people who have found their right place.

Margaret was forty-one, attractive, and unmarried. She was certain that there were no new men worth meeting. She complained that all the men worth meeting already had relationships, had died, or had just been born. She discovered something totally different. She discovered that she did not know how to relate to others in the various life zones.

Joe was thirty-six and certain that the ability to make money was something you were born with. Either you had it or you didn't. And he didn't have it. He discovered something totally different. He hadn't known about the Four Life Zones and how he could be effective in each.

Katherine was fifteen and certain that she wouldn't find friends in her new high school. She felt that she was not pretty enough, smart enough, or athletic enough to attract anyone as her friend. She discovered something totally different. She had been confusing the Four Life Zones and made most of the common mistakes.

Brian, twenty-four, was convinced that he would always be a loser in tennis. He was never going to win the big matches. He thought he would always be a club hacker. He discovered something totally different. He, too, had been suffering from zone confusion.

What did Margaret, Joe, Katherine, and Brian find? They found they were making zone mistakes. And their mistakes put them out of sync. They all changed the way they viewed the world. Instead of seeing one big amorphous world, they now know how to differentiate among the Four Life Zones and make the right connections for each zone. They have become adept at finding personal synchrony. What they have found is something you are learning.

So far in our coaching you have found that to be in sync requires developing your Player Attitude. With your Player Attitude you naturally start making the most of the situation you are in. The next step is learning to relate successfully to the people in your life. It becomes infinitely easier to relate when you know *where* you are with people.

Before we teach you any more about the Four Zones, take the Right Zone Learning Test. This test is designed as a coaching aid to help you learn the differences among the Four Zones, so have a good time taking it. Remember, before we are through with this book, you will have mastered each step.

The Right Zone Learning Test

1. You are in a traffic jam and a cab driver is yelling at you and honking his horn. You start to get upset and have the urge to yell back.

a. You start yelling at him for being so inconsiderate.
b. You get out of the car and explain to him that it's not your fault.
c. You simply wait for the traffic to clear.
d. You look ahead and see what the problem is and decide there is nothing to be done.

The correct answer is (d). You want to be active in the Public Zone without making it a one-on-one event. There are literally hundreds of opportunities to lose in the Public Zone by taking what is happening personally and then blaming yourself or blaming someone else for what is happening. The Public Zone is not personal.

2. You are having dinner with the vice-president of the company you own and he is drinking more than he can handle. When dinner is finished, he wants to drive himself home.
   a. You decide that it's not your problem.
   b. You threaten to fire him if he does drive home.
   c. You call a cab and put him in it.
   d. You drive him home yourself.
   e. Either (c) or (d).

The correct answer is (e). The vice-president is in need of your help. The zone has changed from social to personal. He is not able to help himself. Now is the time to handle the situation. His drinking should not reflect on your opinion of him at work unless his performance is slipping. He may simply have made a mistake. The Personal Zone shows personal vulnerability. We often see that when someone makes a mistake. It is not the time to correct but to assist.

3. You and a friend are having an argument and you can feel yourself getting angry.
   a. You forget it and swallow your anger.
   b. You let yourself go and really get angry.
   c. You tell your friend what is happening and say you need to talk about it.
   d. You decide to let it pass and never to talk about the subject again.

The correct answer is (c). You share what you are feeling as a feeling and not as a fight. A personal friendship is one based on sharing and not on attack and counterattack. The Personal Zone requires vulnerability. In a personal friendship you have let your defenses down with each other; when you are angry, you express it without attack by also expressing your hurt and disappointment and whatever else you are feeling. Remember, in a personal friendship you are vulnerable and so is your friend. Treat vulnerability with care.

4. You are making love with your spouse or lover and you don't feel good.
   a. You get silently angry at your partner for not being a good lover.
   b. You blame yourself for not being sexual enough.
   c. You begin to talk about what is happening to you and how it makes you feel.
   d. You decide to become a Trappist monk.

The correct answer is (c). In this situation you could be in any one of three zones. If you weren't close to begin with, then you were in the Social Zone. If you were talking and revealing your thoughts and feelings, you were in the Personal Zone and you need to keep talking in order to get closer. And if you were intimate with each other by sharing each nuance of the lovemaking, then you were in the Intimate Zone and you certainly would want to continue to talk in order to share more fully yourself and your love. One of the sexiest things people can do is to allow themselves to be emotionally vulnerable while having sex.

5. You and your spouse or date are at a dinner with another couple and they are fighting.
   a. You ask them politely to stop.
   b. You simply smile and hold your mate's hand.
   c. You slowly begin to focus their attention on something outside of themselves.
   d. Both (b) and (c).

The correct answer is (d). Make contact with your own date and then steer the activity toward what is appropriate. Don't make the mistake of getting involved in their problems. This is a Social Zone activity unless you know them really well and they want some help. Even then it is a risky action to take. Remember, in the Social Zone the rewards come from doing. The activity in this case started out to be an enjoyable dinner with another couple.

6. You are working as a consultant, trying to inaugurate a new program at a large company, and a senior division manager is fighting you every step of the way.
   a. You get mad at him and tell his boss what a jerk he is.
   b. You think about it as a game and you learn to get through his defenses.
   c. You think that there must be something wrong with you.
   d. You think that the man should be fired but you worry about getting that involved in company politics.

The correct answer is (b). You play it as a game since it is in the Social Zone. In the Social Zone, especially at work, people lose the playing-it-as-a-game attitude and begin taking what is happening personally. This is a major error in the Social Zone. Whatever you take personally will only come back later to disrupt your drive toward success.

7. You are in your doctor's office and he or she spends a total of 3.5 minutes with you and then gives you a prescription.
   a. You go home and take your medicine, knowing that the good doctor is in charge.
   b. You get mad and change doctors.
   c. You have the nurse call the doctor in and ask him for an explanation of your condition. If need be, you ask for a written report, which you can refer to at home or take to another doctor for a second opinion. You tell the doctor what your needs are, how you need him to treat you, and ask for the time and explanation.
   d. You decide not to go back until you are "really" sick.

The correct answer is (c). Going to the doctor should be a Personal Zone activity. You can't expect your doctor to know how to be personal. He is shifting between the Social Zone, that is, work, and the Personal Zone, that is, his interaction with you. It is up to you to inform him of what you need. If you have personal needs, take the risk of letting the people in your life know about them. If you can show your physician all your private parts, diseases, and warts, you can risk letting him or her know what you think. Take control of this situation or take the consequences of your doctor's controlling it. The choice is yours. When you control, you feel content. If your doctor controls, you may end up feeling like a victim.

8. You arrive at your favorite restaurant and ask for your reservation. The hostess tells you that there is a forty-five minute wait.
   a. You call for the manager and create a stir.
   b. You tell yourself you will never eat there again.
   c. You go into the bar and have a few drinks.
   d. You forget dinner, get mad, and go home.

   The correct answer is (c). This is a social situation and the purpose is sharing the activity. The activity is going out for a good time. It is not the time to start reorganizing the restaurant. Note: A restaurant reservation means only that you will be seated as near to the time set as possible. It doesn't mean that the management kept your table empty for an hour before you arrived. Focus on the main activity of having a good time. Once you know there will be a wait, stop thinking about it and enjoy yourself. You are not going to die of starvation in the meantime. People often make the mistake of thinking that life has to run by *their* clock.

9. You are seeing your therapist and you feel that you are not making progress.
   a. You know the theory—it is probably a resistance on your part—and so you keep silent.
   b. You get angry at the therapist for not knowing what he or she is doing.

c. You start talking about it but expect the therapist to discuss it as if it is solely your problem.

d. You and the therapist talk about it and find out what is happening inside of you and how the therapist thinks about it.

The correct answer is (d). Therapy is about your relationship to yourself and to the therapist. It is a Personal Zone situation. Don't settle for a therapeutic answer. You are not the sick patient waiting for the cure. You are the athlete giving feedback to your coach. A really good therapist relishes hearing what you are really thinking and feeling, because only then can he or she function usefully.

10. Your children are grumpy and causing you trouble.
a. You scream and yell and tell them to get it together.
b. You quietly understand they are growing up.
c. You start talking with them about how you feel about their behavior and how it affects you.
d. You feel sorry you ever had children.

The correct answer is (c). Children are open to your personal and intimate interactions. Many problems children have are signals that they are not getting what they need from you or that they don't know how to get what they need on their own. It is vital to teach children interpersonal (between people) skills and intrapersonal (within themselves) skills in the Personal and Intimate Zones through your behavior with them.

Scoring Results: Let's add up your test results.

10 correct: THE ZONE NATURAL. You have a natural understanding of the Four Life Zones and the rules and regulations for each zone. Use what you know to be more successful in your relationships by teaching others what you know. If you expect them to know what you know, you are going to find yourself disappointed and frustrated.

5–9 correct: ZONE POTENTIAL. You need some coaching on the Four Life Zones. You are probably having relationships that fall into repetitive patterns. It is time to start thinking about those patterns and discover what zone you are experiencing the most trouble in. You will find that with more understanding about each zone, you can change unhappiness and dissatisfaction into joy and satisfaction. No matter how hard you try, you aren't going to succeed if you are in the wrong zone, or in the right zone behaving inappropriately.

0–5 correct: ZONE CONFUSION. Trouble in zone city. There is a good chance that you don't know how to make use of the Four Life Zones. The first thing you need to do is stop looking within yourself for the answer; make the effort to focus outside yourself and learn the regulations of the different zones. If you are having trouble in your relationships and don't know why, it may mean you don't know which zone you are in. You are going to have to start looking at the disconnections, the unhappiness, and the frustration as cues that you are out of sync.

Remember Shelly? She didn't score well at all in the Right Place Learning Test. She didn't know about the Four Life Zones. Like so many people, Shelly looked as if she were winning in the world. All her life Shelly had thought that when she had what she now had, she would be happy. She is no different from any one of us. Many people think that *when* they pay off their MasterCard balance, redecorate the house, get the new job, lose the fifteen pounds, *then* they will be happy. (Or a prize notion: "I'll feel better when *you* change.")

Shelly had reached a point where the picture looked perfect from the outside. Still she was unhappy. It was a wrong-place situation. For example, when she came home from work to be with her husband and family, she was entering the Personal Zone, but she kept using the work (a Social Zone) rules and regulations. It was no wonder she was having so many problems. To find the right place you have to ask yourself Question Number One: "Where am I right now?" To ask this question means you have started to use your Player Attitude. If you are using a Nonplayer Attitude, you won't even take the time to ask, "Where am I right now?" Instead, you just plow ahead, hoping everything will

turn out the way you want it to. It won't. Otherwise, you would
have a history of successful relationships. Put your Player Attitude to work and ask Question Number One: "Where am I right
now?" If you know where you are, you can start off in the right
direction.

We live in a society where people try to make it appear that
everything is all right. We try to act as if we don't need anything
from anyone else, that we always know what we are doing. If
people knew what zone they were in, they would know what
leads to success instead of defending positions that aren't giving
them the satisfaction they want in the first place.

Are You Suffering from Zone Confusion?

Many of Shelly's problems were the result of not knowing
when or how to shift among the different zones. She would complete a big deal at work one day and feel great. She would be
speaking quickly and matter-of-factly, moving decisively. And
then she would go home and forget to switch to the Personal
Zone, which requires vulnerability, time, and sharing. Emotionally, she would crash into her husband because she was moving at an entirely different speed. More often than not, she would
wind up fighting with him simply because she didn't know how
to switch zones. She was suffering from zone confusion but she
didn't know it. She thought there was something wrong with her.
At other times she would have a close personal weekend with
her family and the next Monday morning take that personal feeling to work. When she felt personal at work she would take the
more distant and impersonal work interactions as signals to
worry that she was doing something wrong. Sound confused?
She was.

Knowing about the four zones is only the beginning of creating
the right place. The question is, how do you do it? In the introduction I described the personal-coaching method of change as a
three-part process. STEP ONE is to work to change how you view
the world—as you see it. You change perception with new information and by putting that new information into action. If you
can learn to perceive the different zones you will be startled at
how naturally you will begin to interact with people. You will

know why, where, and how you used to fail, how you can now succeed, and how you can make the connections that bring you satisfaction. Here is what John learned.

John was a client who was artistically rich and financially poor. He painted wonderful abstract paintings and he had a total commitment to his art. The only problem was that he never sold any paintings. He had talent. He would win art shows and get critical acclaim, but if someone wanted to buy one of his paintings and didn't understand the meaning of the painting, John wouldn't sell it. Not enough people were passing his tests of artistic understanding to enable him to make a living. John was waiting tables at night to support his painting. When he reached thirty-four, he decided something had to change, and he thought about getting out of painting. What was happening was that John was confusing two different zones. When he was painting in his SoHo studio, he was in the Personal Zone. He had strong emotional reactions to his work and was thoughtful about life and life's meaning. But selling a painting is not a Personal Zone activity. It is a Social Zone activity. John learned to differentiate between the two zones and eventually found he liked earning money from his work.

To enrich your perspective you have to make an effort to notice the different life zones. The effort to notice also impugns your old way of looking at the world. In the sections that follow, there are many different clues and signs to help you identify each zone. The more you use them, the more quickly you will develop the ability to spot the different zones. Once you have developed the ability to differentiate among them, you are going to have *new action opportunities.*

STEP TWO is to seize those new action opportunities. Even if what you attempt doesn't turn out the way you wanted, you have to give it a try, and keep on trying.

Susan is a thirty-year-old bank executive. One night she and her boyfriend were having an especially intimate and personal time. They were discussing very revealing and hidden parts of their lives and then suddenly they seemed to crash. Abruptly, Susan's boyfriend got up and said that he had to go. Susan had developed the ability to perceive the Four Zones; she knew they were in the Personal Zone and he had become vulnerable. Her old way of handling this kind of situation would have been to feel hurt, display anger, and wind up dissatisfied. Instead, she seized this new action opportunity. She stood up and said, "You aren't going anywhere. You just became overly sensitive. If you want to have a relationship with me, you have to be willing to share what you are feeling with me." Her lover looked at her in stunned silence. She had hit the nail on the head. He had walked out on dozens of women and never had any one of them say what Susan had said. He stopped in his tracks and sat back down. They both laughed and continued their discussion. Susan had made the most of the situation she was in. She had created the right place. Susan had learned how to do this by changing her perception and responding to her new action opportunities. She herself created the result she had sought all her life.

Perception and action lead to STEP THREE, which is new consequences. When a new consequence occurs you have to identify it and know how you made it happen through your change in perception and action. The more successful your relationships, the better you are going to feel about yourself. On the other hand, poor connections with other people cause stress, illness, and a loss of self-esteem. The previously mentioned report by the California Department of Mental Health noted: "Compared with people who maintain supportive relationships, socially isolated persons have *2–3 times* the overall *risk of dying* prematurely." There is other evidence that shows successful people and happy people are those who have good relationships with others. Harvard researcher George Vaillant reports that the most successful people were those with positive connections to the people in their lives. Researcher Norman Bradburn studied the components of psychological health and reported in his book *The Structure of Psychological Well-Being* findings similar to Vaillant's. *The evidence is clear—how you feel about yourself is very much determined by how well you relate to people.* Often we fail to relate well to people unless the "circumstances" are just right. Being in the right place is not dependent on your mood or on what is happening *inside* you. You can start to feel terrible and yet succeed if you make the effort to focus on what life zone you are in and what is appropriate for that zone.

Loretta is a horse trainer. The horse-show circuit is a highly political arena where it often matters more whom you know and who knows you than how good your horse is. The politics so infuriated Loretta that her concentration frequently broke while she was showing a horse. We had been working together to help her take control of this overreaction because it was keeping her from performing at her best.

It happened one day at the Denver stock show. She had just watched a class go before her. The favorite won, but Loretta was convinced one of the lesser-known riders had done much better. It was time for her to show in the next class, but she was so agitated that when she got on her horse he sensed it and started to spook. Then it hit her. She said:

"I finally got to see it in action. My reactions were turning my best horse into a nut. He was doing things he had never done before. And then all the work we had done on staying focused on the outside made sense. At that moment it didn't matter what I thought about the judges or the last class. What mattered was what I had to do. I went out and did better than I had ever done. I focused on what I had to do and the anger just left me. I know how to win now."

Loretta is a winner because she knows *when* to focus on the outside. *No matter how much inner understanding, insight, and sensitivity you have about yourself, there comes a time when your self-esteem, your satisfaction, and your good feelings come from how you are with other people.* You don't have to like everyone you meet or everyone you deal with, but to be in the right place you have to give your best to the interactions in your life. Otherwise, you find yourself continually searching for the "right person" or the "right situation" in order to be successful.

Other people are your life teammates—some are good and some are poor, but they are your teammates for as long as you are with them. You don't get to relate to other people just when the fancy strikes you, or only when you feel like it, or when the sun is shining. If you are going to interact, then interact at your best when it is happening. And when it is happening, it is always "game time." But always remember: In any interaction with other people—no matter how much you explain, communicate, and connect—there will be misunderstanding, miscommunication, and misperception. All the glitches, hurt feelings, and miscues are part and parcel of human interaction. The more you learn about the four zones, the sooner you stop searching inside yourself for answers that, in fact, lie in understanding how to interact successfully in life.

Let me show you, zone by zone, what I taught Shelly.

CHAPTER

·4·

The Misunderstood Public Zone

The Public Zone is the most abused, and misunderstood of the Four Life Zones. When I work with clients, they all seem to want to go straightway into the Intimate Zone. They want to know about love and intimacy, how to get to the nitty-gritty of life. To develop satisfying and long-term relationships requires that you start and be successful in the Public Zone. The Public Zone is full of excitement and variety, novelty and participation.

I have coached more people out of loneliness and depression by showing them how to get into the Public Zone than by discovering what went wrong at age five. When you feel depressed or lonely, you are frequently sitting by yourself. You may not know it, but you have lost perspective on the rest of the world and your place in it. When you get out into the Public Zone, you start to find that your problems or even your successes are not as big and as important as you might have believed. In the Public Zone you are part of the crowd, one of the gang. If you can learn the give-and-take, the push-and-pull of the Public Zone, you are going to find yourself able to keep your intimate relationships alive and much more satisfying.

It was the work of the anthropologist Edward Hall that provided the necessary ingredient for any understanding of the right place. He originally developed the concepts of the four zones from his work in anthropology. I blended his work into my coaching methods to help you find the right place. The four zones are connected to each other like links in a chain. If one link is weak, the entire chain is weak. Each of the four zones has different behaviors, feelings, and attitudes, which are peculiar to that zone. If you know what zone you are in, then you know what is appropriate and what is not. *Knowing what zone you are in and when to shift zones is another step toward the right place.*

Clues for Finding the Right Place in the Public Zone

As you learned earlier, the outermost life zone, and the easiest to understand, is called the Public Zone. You are in the Public Zone when you are doing something or going somewhere and the situation is *impersonal.* You are there to make brief connections with people. In the Public Zone anyone has the same right to be there as you do. Interactions in which you experience *brief,* often one-time, *encounters* with strangers, waitresses, clerks, or passersby occur here. It could be a nod to a passing stranger on the street, a smile in a crowded elevator, courtesy to the person in the car next to you on the freeway during rush hour, cheering with the crowd at a baseball game, or sharing the wait with fellow travelers in the airport lobby during a snowstorm. Remember, the interactions are going to be brief, so you have to pay attention to catch them.

You are in the right place in the Public Zone when you know what zone you are in and you interact at that level. You are in the Public Zone when you are driving down the freeway, walking down the street, riding a bus, shopping, attending a political meeting, listening to a concert. If you react personally to what is happening, or if someone cuts you off on the freeway and you start yelling and give chase with your car—you are suffering from zone confusion. If you expect everyone at a baseball game to conform to your manners, you are suffering from zone confusion. You have no control over events in the Public Zone; you have control over *yourself* in the event. Most people don't know how to get the most from the Public Zone and therefore miss out on one quarter of their lives.

Yaron was a very successful broker but he never knew what to do with his off time. He just sat alone in his apartment. He thought that he wasn't good-looking enough or interesting enough for women to like him. Sometimes he thought that if a woman did like him he'd get bored. He was out of sync, living in an unreal world of his mind's invention.

I knew that Yaron would never find out what to do by sitting in his apartment. To help him find the right place, I helped him to interpret the tremendous amount of information available in the Public Zone. Once he knew where things were happening, he started going to those places where he felt the most comfortable. At first he came home feeling disappointed. He learned to stay in the game by giving himself more time in the Public Zone. When you remain in the Public Zone for a while, things begin to happen. Opportunities emerge and new action becomes possible.

COACH'S NOTE

Instruction in personal synchrony should start in the Public Zone. There are fewer risks. Strangers appear and disappear rapidly. Experiment and master the Public Zone before going on to the Social Zone. Remember, we aren't trying to finish anything but rather to build a foundation. If you take your time now, you will reap greater benefits later.

Yaron learned to acknowledge people's smiles, the invitations to talk, the warm glances. He found himself in sync by getting *out into the world* and making Public Zone connections. It may sound simple to you, but getting out into the Public Zone was a giant step for Yaron. He found there were many people out there who had a lot to offer and who wanted what he had to offer.

Ellen had been married for twenty-six years and always argued about the same thing with her husband, Sol. She wanted to go out and he wanted to stay home. She began to question the marriage itself. Ellen loved concerts and plays. Sol always found excuses not to go.

Although he insisted that he could get the rest he needed only by staying home, what he really needed was the change of perspective and the excitement that the Public Zone offered.

Ellen and Sol fought because they didn't know how to use the Public Zone. Ellen was the one who took action. She and I spent time creating a chart of New York's different cultural activities. The more she took control over her actions in the Public Zone, the more choices she had and the clearer she became about what she and her husband needed. They discovered they loved going to off-Broadway plays by unknown writers. Once Sol discovered that he did not have to hassle with the traffic and crowds, he got excited about exploring the Public Zone with Ellen. They satisfied their need for cultural stimulation without succumbing to the rat race of midtown Broadway.

In the Public Zone Shelly was out of sync and didn't know why. For example, whenever she was out among strangers she acted very aloof and preoccupied. She was misreading the zone. You cannot satisfy your Public Zone needs by being aloof and preoccupied. She was clearly out of sync.

Shelly used to be so wrapped up in herself she had no time for a smile or common courtesy in the Public Zone. Because she failed to break out of her cocoon, she was not experiencing the wonderful excitement, freshness, change of perspective, and sense of being part of a larger whole. In the Public Zone, it is the event that is the focus of attention. You are in the right place in the Public Zone when you focus on what is happening outside of you. Places and positions quickly shift in the Public Zone and you need to pay attention to what is happening to discover what the Public Zone has to offer. You are in the wrong place when you sit at home thinking about your problems. At home alone, it is as if everyone and everything in the universe is focused on you. When you get out into the Public Zone, you find out right away you are simply a member of the human race and not the star (or goat) of the show. So many people make the mistake of telling themselves that they will go public when they feel better or feel more comfortable. But it is precisely small forays into the Public Zone that make you feel comfortable. Remember, the Public Zone is there with rewards of an unexpected and unusual character. You don't dress up in your favorite robe and slippers. What's appropriate are tennis shoes, sunglasses, and exploration. *When you go out, go out to be in the Public Zone, not to race through it.* To find the Public Zone rewards you have to put yourself in it.

As a coach I am interested in how clients do in the real world. One of the ways I find this out is by going for walks with them. Shelly and I spent hours walking around in the Public Zone, watching and discussing what was happening. I got her to tell me about what she felt and what she thought was going on. Very often she took what was happening as personal. She found the right place in the Public Zone by recognizing that the situation was impersonal but that it required her assertive and energetic attitude to get what it had to offer. Once she could identify the times and places when she was in the Public Zone, she no longer reacted as personally to the cab driver whose music was too loud or who was smoking his cigarette. Instead, she took action without the emotion of the Personal Zone. She felt better because she had changed her perception of the Public Zone and subsequently she saw it as a friendlier place. She had learned how to fulfill her needs in the Public Zone.

If she was at the store and the game was "shopping," then winning was easy. She no longer treated clerks like inconveniences; instead, she was friendly, smiled, got them to play the shopping game with her. And when she was traveling and the game was "travel," she no longer treated flight attendants and fellow passengers as if they were the cause of every mishap, inconvenience, or delay. Shelly simply played the travel game for what it was—a Public Zone event.

COACH'S NOTE: PUBLIC ZONE RULES AND REGULATIONS

PUBLIC ZONE: The main rules of the Public Zone are to have a friendly demeanor and not take what is happening personally. Most people you encounter in the Public Zone you will never encounter again, and it is vital to make the most of what does happen. You can smile, you can say hello, you can make a comment. It is amazing with how many people you might have that momentary human connection in the Public Zone, and yet don't. Your action in the low-risk Public Zone will train you for taking action in the higher-risk Social, Personal, and Intimate Zones. The main regulation is to *explore* new ideas, new places, new people, and new events. And you need to be active and friendly. When you allow yourself the freedom to enjoy your *right* to the Public Zone, you find that the world is bigger than you ever imagined. To get the most out of the Public Zone, don't take the traffic jam, the honking horns, the smog, the crowd in the park as personal.

They are part of the public territory. But more than that, you have to get out into the Public Zone—you have to go and find what the Public Zone has to offer you. The key to getting what the Public Zone has to offer is active participation. If you follow the simple steps for the Public Zone, you will have begun knowing how to create the right place.

In Chapter Five we are going to find out about the Social Zone. But before we do, let's review the Public Zone. The Public Zone is where you make connection through the event. If you want to integrate what you have learned about the Public Zone, you are going to have to take some new action. When you go out into the Public Zone, think about the rules and regulations for success. Remember, knowing about the Public Zone is not the same as practicing the changes so that you can be successful in it. To be successful you have to take action.

Common Public Zone Mistakes

Shyness: Shyness occurs when you are using the rules and regulations of the Personal and Intimate Zones in the Public Zone. You are reacting to strangers as if they were personal friends. Remember, the person you think cares about you in the Public Zone is merely passing by. He or she doesn't have time to wonder about you.

Work: To have a successful business, you have to know how to communicate with people in the Public Zone. At work you have to help people discover you. Make yourself available to others at work. This means listening to what people need and want and filling that need. In the Public Zone, what you communicate has to be fresh, new, and stimulating. People communicate in the Public Zone through what they wear, how they carry themselves, and how confidently they interact. Make sure you are furthering your career by your Public Zone messages.

Family: To maintain your family as a unit, you need to take the family out into the Public Zone together. This allows the family a sense of identity—here we are and there is the world.

Fear: The Public Zone has become a fearful place for many people. You become afraid when you don't know how to relate in the Public Zone. Act like a victim and you are going to attract victimizers. Protect yourself by learning what you need to do to stay healthy and happy in the Public Zone and then go about your business. Don't become a bystander in your Public Zone out of fear.

Relationships: Relationships fall into ruts because once a couple find each other, they often stop exploring the Public Zone. If that is happening to you, take your mate and start exploring what is possible for the two of you to discover. The Public Zone is where you find those new experiences that bring you closer together.

COACH'S NOTES

1. In the Public Zone you have to let yourself be noticed and actively notice other people. Remember that the Public Zone is about "out there," not inside of you.
2. Don't wait to take action until you feel good.
3. Change occurs when you become aware of your old behaviors and feelings. It is the lack of awareness that reinforces the old patterns.
4. The more you learn about the four zones, the more you are going to discover just how afraid other people are. They are afraid because they are lost. They don't know one zone from another. You can stop treating other people as if they have power you don't have. Right now, with what you know, you have power.
5. If you want to find friends, lovers, and connections, start in the Public Zone. It doesn't mean you go out looking; instead, it means you go out participating in the world. If you know how to participate, your chances of getting invited into the more intimate zones goes up.

CHAPTER
·5·

The Social Zone:
It's Not Personal

I n the Public Zone, whatever is happening—the concert, the parade, the window-shopping—is the central focus. But in the Social Zone—it is what you *do* that takes center stage.

Jennifer was one of the hottest young advertising account executives in the business. But she never made it to the top. She had the talent, but there was something keeping her from success—the fact that she took her performance personally. She thought that how she played was a statement about her worth as a person. She was confusing the Social Zone with the Personal Zone.

In the Social Zone you have permission to try, to go for your very best, to fail and keep trying. You don't have to make excuses or compare yourself to anyone else in the Social Zone.

You are in the Social Zone when the ACTIVITY you are doing is the main focus. It is any interaction that involves work, sports, movies, dinners, vacations, parties, or doing something. In the Social Zone you spend more time with the people you are with, while in the Public Zone there is a *momentary connection* with people. You are in the Social Zone wherever and whenever people share an activity but there is little risk to emotional vulnerabilities. You create the right place in the Social Zone when you participate and hold up your end of the activity. If you use the Public Zone rules and behavior or the Personal and Intimate rules and behavior, you are in the wrong place.

Let's take a closer look at what several people discovered about the Social Zone.

Robert was an insurance adjuster. And work for him was stressful. He munched antacid tablets all day long. By the time he got home he felt exhausted and yet unable to unwind. Most of the stress was caused by reactions to the people with whom he worked. He kept trying to analyze what was wrong with them and to understand what was wrong with himself. But what was really wrong was that he didn't know that work took place in the Social Zone. He reacted as if it were personal. Whenever one of Robert's subordinates made a mistake, Robert used to get angry and become very punishing. After a lot of coaching, Robert found that he was reacting as if their mistakes were directed against him, rather than accepting that they simply didn't know how to do something. And when he found that someone consistently did something wrong and didn't want to learn something new, he could calmly fire him or her.

On the other hand, whenever Robert made a mistake, he used to think that his superiors were angry with him. With his superiors he was doing to himself what he did to employees—reacting personally. He would often feel that he had overreacted with his employees and he would worry about it for days. And if Robert had gotten disapproval from his superiors, he would fear that more was on its way. He spent much too much time worrying, time that could have been spent working toward more success.

Robert and I spent hours going over the Social Zone and what was really happening in it. Slowly, he began to understand just how personal he had made the Social Zone. He began to catch himself when he started to get angry or thought his superiors were angry with him, and before long he wasn't feeling stress at work. He gave up his worry and judgments and focused on how to succeed. He changed his focus from personal to performance. He became a player at work instead of judge and jury.

Marlene was a well-known actress who was very successful at work, but she continually complained about how "meaningless" cocktail parties were. She felt trapped in a bind because she had to go to a lot of parties for her work. She kept saying she wanted people to be "real" at parties. Marlene would be critical and bitchy at the parties she did attend because in her mind other people deserved it for being so superficial. When she finally learned about the Four Life Zones, she realized she was trying to do the impossible—to get a personal friendship connection from the Social Zone.

What was really happening was that Marlene was so busy she was suffering from Personal Zone deprivation. Her need for personal contact and connection was so great that she was desperate. She was putting herself in the wrong place. To get in the right place, she did two things: She started taking more personal time to get her personal needs met, and she carefully chose the parties she went to. Once she accepted an invitation, she made the most of it by being outgoing, friendly, and taking the risk of getting to know new people. She didn't wait for the party to happen, she did her part. She no longer had to drink that extra drink to get herself going.

Shelly had both success and failure in the Social Zone. She got her rewards of respect, success, and money by effectively playing the "work game." She was good at work because she could concentrate on the particular project she was working on, communicate well with others, and give lots of feedback about progress on the project. But Shelly spent so much time and energy on work, she had little time or energy for the Personal and Intimate Zones. Many people forget that the Personal and Intimate Zones require as much energy as the Social Zone. Not spending enough time in the Personal and the Intimate Zone will produce depression, unhappiness, and dissatisfaction. It is odd that we don't save much energy for those we want the most from—our family, mates, lovers, and friends.

Shelly was trying to get more from work than it could give her. As she learned to identify the Social Zone, she learned that work was about activity and not about her as a person. Shelly stopped making each work project a statement about her personal worth. The success or failure of a project no longer meant she was a good or bad person. Shelly stopped worrying and began using that "worry energy" to produce better results.

She really started winning at work when she found herself standing up for a project she had worked on. One of the senior executives who was continually putting Shelly down started in on one of her projects during the weekly staff meeting. Instead of meekly stepping back, Shelly asked him, "What is it that you don't like about the project?" He didn't have an answer. And so Shelly seized the opportunity. "I can understand what your objections might be with a quick read, but I think you will find upon closer study that we have covered ourselves and our client's best interests with my proposal." Shelly had done it. Everyone looked at her differently. She knew how to win in the Social Zone. She was assertive; she stood up for herself without getting into the trap of defending against the executive's attack. What follows are the Social Zone rules and regulations to help you do the same.

COACH'S NOTES: SOCIAL ZONE RULES AND REGULATIONS

SOCIAL ZONE: The main regulation for the Social Zone is wholehearted and active participation. And the main rule is not to take the action personally. In any activity there are different perceptions, misperceptions, and close calls. Don't get stuck trying to have the Social Zone go your way all the time. Instead, focus on making the activity in the Social Zone effective. You win in the Social Zone by getting to be the best you can be at what you are doing, not by controlling anyone else.

You succeed in the Social Zone when you give your best at work.

You succeed in the Social Zone when you try your hardest during a ski weekend.

You succeed in the Social Zone when you let yourself make mistakes because you are trying new activities.

You succeed in the Social Zone when you talk, laugh, and enliven whatever event you are at.

You succeed in the Social Zone when you make work as exciting as a championship game.

You succeed in the Social Zone when you let yourself learn new skills from other people.

You succeed in the Social Zone when you express your appreciation for the performance skills of other people.

The key characteristic of the Social Zone is *DOING*. When you start to do something—then do it. You may not like it or ever want to do it again—but when you are doing it is not the time to complain and be negative. *The Social Zone is the place that allows you to enjoy yourself in action.* Remember, exercising choice leads to contentment. You have a choice each and every moment of your life.

Competition: In the Social Zone you are going to have to compete. The secret of success is not to compete against someone else but against your best. If you perform at your best, and block out what others are doing, you will find that you don't make the mistakes that lead to failure. Instead, you will find that you become consistently good. Don't play to the level of the competition; play to the level of your potential.

Opposition: In the Social Zone, each step of the way there is going to be opposition. Imagine a football game without a defensive team. There would be no game. Don't fight your opposition, understand it. Don't expect to be understood. Your job in the Social Zone is to win by playing to your potential.

Hierarchy: In the Social Zone there are hierarchies. Learn what they are. Don't spend your time changing them; spend your time moving up and through them. Your job is to perform at your best in the situation you are in. The more time you spend complaining, the less time you have to focus on your success. Remember, the only people who have time to listen to your complaints are those who aren't in power but would like to be.

Mistakes: In the Social Zone there is no "best" way of doing anything. There is only getting the job done. If your boss or someone else is making a mistake—get out of the way. Don't confront someone else's stupidity. And when you make a mistake—get out of your own way. Don't carry your mistake with you forever. Think about John McEnroe and Bjorn Borg. No matter what McEnroe did, he couldn't beat Borg at Wimbledon. If he was still focused on his losses, he wouldn't be the champion he is today.

Winning: Be careful *what* you try to get. You just might get it. In the Social Zone, don't waste your time winning arguments that don't lead to real success. No one cares if you are right and unsuccessful. Make sure what you go after is what you want.

Connecting: You connect with people in the Social Zone

through what you are doing. If you give 100 percent of yourself to what you are doing in the Social Zone, you are going to make an impression on people even when you don't know it. Stay with giving your all; it pays off in the long run. People will feel good connecting with you.

Player Attitude: There is no better place to use your Player Attitude than in the Social Zone. Use it at work, with your co-workers, and with the people you play with. Your Player Attitude shows people you are here to play. You aren't sitting on the side-lines of life.

COACH'S NOTES:

1. How you relate to people is not a statement about your personal worth; it is simply what you have learned. Given new information, you can be different.
2. It is not important how you have been, but how you want to be. Let your goals guide you.
3. You can be guaranteed that *everyone* you interact with will at some time be irrational—but they can change from irrational to rational if you don't overreact to the irrational. A person is irrational when he or she is acting from memory and not in the present. What a person remembers is an old drama. You create the right place in an irrational interaction by not taking it personally and by staying in the present.
4. Don't base your decisions on what others are doing or not doing but on the knowledge of *what zone* you are in and the *goals* you have. Move toward what you know is the best you can do.
5. Human interaction is fairly consistent. Scout yourself, your teammates, and your opponents for the strengths and weaknesses in the four zones. Find out what zones you and others make your most frequent mistakes in and what zones you are the best in. Keep your Player Attitude so that you don't take zone weaknesses as a sign of failure.
6. Don't wait until you feel good to take action.
7. Boredom and dissatisfaction are hints that your needs are not being met in your relationships. It's easy to blame others. Your dissatisfaction doesn't mean someone is doing some-

thing wrong; it just means it is time for you to start doing
something new and right.

8. Change occurs when you become aware of your old behaviors and feelings. It is the lack of awareness that reinforces the old patterns.

9. Many people think they are shy in the Social Zone. Shyness is
usually a simple lack of skills. It's much easier to learn some
new skills than to get over shyness.

10. Anxiety is withheld action. Use your anxiety as a cue for
identifying what zone you are in and as a clue for what action you need to take.

Shelly was good at creating the right place in the Social Zone.
But when it came time to be personal, it was a different story.
Let's see what the Personal Zone is all about.

When It's Time to Let Down the Walls: The Personal Zone

Heart. The Personal Zone requires heart. There is no zone people want more and have a harder time finding than the Personal Zone. In the Personal Zone friendships are made and kept. And in the Personal Zone you are able to discover what you are like without its having anything to do with your performance.

You are in sync in the Personal Zone when what you are doing takes second place to the EXPERIENCE of doing it with someone else. The *rewards* of the Personal Zone are those moments of feeling connected, close, and free with another person. You create the right place in the Personal Zone when and where you and another *share* much of *yourselves* in a heartfelt way. Many people make the mistake of taking the Personal Zone for granted. They don't take the time or make the effort to increase their expertise and satisfaction.

You are in sync in the Personal Zone when you are vulnerable. Vulnerability is the signal that says we don't have to do anything, be anybody, to be together. We are just here, you and I, as we are. It takes self-worth to let someone else know you are hurting, to let someone else see your weaknesses and care for you. But that is what makes the right place in the Personal Zone so satisfying.

People want the rewards of the Personal Zone but often don't know how to get them. Let's find out what these people learned.

Bob was in his third year of medical school. He spent so much time studying that he didn't have much left for his personal needs. When he and I first started talking, he was wondering if medical school was worth all the effort. I guessed that his personal needs were not being met. He needed a big dose of human contact, which comes from the Personal Zone. Bob and I started talking about friends. He told me about his best friend from college who was living in Philadelphia. I asked how much they talked and he said twice a year. The more he talked about his friend, the clearer it became that he had a wonderful personal relationship but he wasn't taking the time to get the rewards it had to offer. Bob learned that to be in the right place in the Personal Zone meant calling and setting aside time for friendship. He was surprised to find that his friend was willing to come down once a month and visit when Bob took study breaks. For Bob to find the right place in the Personal Zone meant pulling down his facade and letting another person get close to him.

What frequently goes wrong in the Personal Zone is that people take their personal relationships for granted. If there was an Olympic event for the Personal Zone, we all know the winner would be the one who practiced every day and never took his or her relationship for granted. The Personal Zone requires art, skill, practice, heart, and instinct. If you don't know how to be personally effective, you can learn. If you take your personal relationships for granted, problems are a natural consequence. A family lives in the Personal Zone. The family requires teammates, teamwork, and team play. When something is wrong with someone in a family, it is everyone's problem. And yet we often react as if it were someone else's problem, not our problem.

It is not difficult to fail in the Personal Zone. You just have to take it for granted. My clients do that all the time. One family in particular comes to mind. They were a basically loving family of five, the parents and three teenaged children. For them it was either feast or famine. They would spend holidays together, but the rest of the time everyone was too busy for family. They came to me because Julie, the middle daughter, was having a problem with her eating. The family rallied around, helping Julie get through her mild case of anorexia, but it took them by surprise when I told them that I thought they were all starving. During our coaching they began to see that Julie's anorexia was not just her problem but a symbol of how little personal satisfaction any of the family members had. As we worked together they decided to start taking time just to be with one another, to share what they were thinking and feeling, and not to wait until the next big problem or holiday occurred.

People succeed in the Personal Zone when they are sharing their worries, their fears, their joys, in a self-exposing way. There is no right way or my way or this way. There is only a sharing of the difficulty of living life in a complex and changing society. The barriers that normally come between people come down in the Personal Zone. You are making the most of the Personal Zone when *you can feel* yourself letting down your barriers and setting aside defenses with someone else so that you are consciously taking a risk. Being in sync in the Personal Zone is a little scary because it is so different from the Social and Public Zones. What worked in those zones doesn't work in the Personal Zone. In fact, you wind up in the wrong place if you use the Public and Social Zone rules and regulations in the Personal Zone.

In the Personal Zone you can get hurt because as you open up with another person you may hit his or her inner stone wall. You may have made an error in judgment when someone you thought was personal turned out not to be. But you will make a worse mistake if you never take the risk of entering into the Personal Zone. It is worth the risk because it is only in the Personal Zone that you get that special connection between you and another person. In the Personal Zone you *talk about yourself* rather than about events, gossip, or familiar stories. There is an open-endedness about what is happening.

Success in the Personal Zone is available to those people who are willing to be vulnerable and open with each other. *In the Personal Zone no one is in control over what is said and no one has the upper hand.* Success in the Personal Zone is a give-and-take affair between two equals. It is two unique human beings being together.

Shelly had many problems in the Personal Zone. For her to win in the Personal Zone meant her connections with her husband and children had to be based on feelings and understanding. As Shelly and I talked, she recalled the time she had yelled at Matthew and he ran into his room crying. It was an extremely difficult step for Shelly to admit she needed to learn how to be personal. She kept feeling guilty about hurting Matthew's feelings rather than accepting her mistake and going on to take new action. She put herself in sync with Matthew when she walked into his room one day and sat on his bed. "Matthew," she said, "I want to talk to you about the time I screamed at you." "Oh, it's all right, Mom." "No, it wasn't, Matt, I was wrong, and I know I hurt your feelings." Matthew's eyes started to tear. "Mom, it doesn't matter." "Matt, it matters because I am changing and I want you to know how I want things to be. I want you to be able to tell me when I hurt your feelings. Sometimes I get so wound up from work I blow up and take it out on you or Karen. I want us all to keep our loving and sweet feelings." Matthew turned and reached out to Shelly. They had found their Personal Zone. What Shelly was able to do with Matthew, she did with her daughter and her husband. Not just once, but as a matter of habit. Shelly learned to listen to other people in the Personal Zone and to respond to what they were saying rather than waiting to tell her next story or whatever was on her mind. She found that the Personal Zone required she give her attention to others and ask them to pay attention to her. This newfound Personal Zone sensitivity filled many of Shelly's deepest needs.

COACH'S NOTE:

Some people are naturally very sensitive to others. They have an interpersonal intelligence. For the rest of the world, it is something that can be learned. When you meet others who have this special intelligence, study them, learn from them and follow their emotional lead.

The more time Shelly took with her family and friends, the better the communication, the less fighting, and the fewer disagreements she had. And she found more personal happiness. She started feeling better about herself and the people in her life. Before she learned these skills, Shelly felt out of place in the Personal Zone. And instead of staying where she felt uncomfortable, she would continually go back to work in the Social Zone where she knew what to do. By going back to work, Shelly was keeping herself from filling her personal needs. No matter how much success she had at work, it couldn't give her enough success to make up for her failure in her personal interactions. Shelly was lonely because people couldn't get through to her in the Personal Zone. To be personal meant Shelly had to be willing to hear what people had to say to her without defending her position. It didn't mean others were right or that she had to change; it was simply the requirement for successful interaction in the Personal Zone.

COACH'S NOTES: PERSONAL ZONE RULES AND REGULATIONS

PERSONAL ZONE: The main rules and regulations of the Personal Zone are openness and risk taking. This means you talk person to person about what you think, feel, and do. You are vulnerable and there is no right or wrong, guilt or judgment—there is only the working through of the stages and situations of life. The Personal Zone is where you risk saying the thoughts that aren't neatly packaged in a story, expressing the feelings that reveal your vulnerability and need, and doing the things that are new and unfamiliar.

If you are personal you are willing to confront directly.

If you are personal you are willing to support unilaterally.

If you are personal you are willing to give advice.

If you are personal you are willing to take advice.

If you are personal you are willing to expose your weaknesses.

If you are personal you are willing to say to someone else what you usually keep to yourself.

Relationships: You can't have a personal relationship with merely the time left over from work. It takes as much energy to have a contented relationship as it does to keep your job. Most personal relationships survive on the fragments of energy and good feelings that are left over from all the other activities. A good relationship isn't a mystery; it is the result of dedication to that relationship.

Attitude: In the Personal Zone attitude is paramount. If you or someone you are personal with has a Nonplayer Attitude, then you are eroding whatever personal satisfaction you could get. A personal relationship demands that both people have Player Attitudes. This means there is no blaming, neither one is better than the other, and no one is in control over the other. In the Personal Zone—there is equality.

Time: The Personal Zone requires time—the time to settle into each other's rhythm, and the time to synchronize emotions. When you want to be personal, you have to cut out any interference. Otherwise, your outside world will pollute your personal relationship. Don't get talked out of what it means to be personal.

The key characteristic of the Personal Zone is your goodwill. You are willing to try to understand what is beyond your experience. You are willing to experiment with change through new ideas, new influences, and new information.

COACH'S NOTES:

1. To change you have to listen to what other people have to say, even though what they have to say is often wrong. You benefit by sitting through what they say. Listen not only to *what* a person says but *how* he says it.

2. Relationships take place in all four zones—the key is knowing how and when to be in each of the four zones.

3. By practicing new behavior you can actually change the quality of your relationships.

4. A relationship is like a river. If you merely float, it will take you where it will, usually into the past of each person where irrational behaviors and childhood feelings lie in wait. But if you take up the oars and pull on them, the relationship will acquire an energy and direction of its own. Through your action you can tap the energy of the relationship and use it to satisfy your needs. And you need a constant source of energy to make the most of your potential.

5. To change a relationship requires that *you acknowledge when you don't know what to do.* When you are at the point of not knowing what to do and you do what is familiar, you will be repeating a failure pattern. You change when you admit "I don't know what to do" and let yourself live with the unfamiliar. Your experience in the unfamiliar will teach you what to do because it opens you to new choices.

6. Relationships work or don't work depending on whether you know where you are with people. If you don't know where you are, you can be certain that you will be plagued with mutual misunderstandings, misinterpretations, and misconceptions.

7. Don't base your decisions on what others are doing or not doing but on the knowledge of *what zone* you are in and the *goals* you have. Move toward the best you can do.

8. If you think you should be mad, upset, or hurt because of what someone else has done, you are falling into a relationship trap. You are acting out a role in a play you haven't written—but are getting ready to star in. Stop. You can rewrite the play and star in a different way—a successful way—a contented way.

9. Accept the fact that most human interaction is filled with miscommunication, misunderstanding, and misperception. If you want to be successful, you have to stop taking all the *mis*es personally.

10. Human interaction is fairly consistent. Scout yourself, your teammates, and your opponents for the strengths and weaknesses in the four zones. Find out what zones you and others make your mistakes in and what zones you are the best in. Keep your Player Attitude so that you don't take zone weaknesses as a sign of failure.

11. Know when it is time for a relationship time-out (that is, maintaining a friendly, positive distance) and a relationship game time (getting closer to each other).

12. You can't stand up for yourself and be against someone and still have a satisfying relationship. You have to learn to stand up for yourself in relationships without being against someone else.

13. Relationships are like plays or movies or books—they can be edited and rewritten to satisfy needs. You don't have to live by the present picture of the relationship. Have the courage to admit when you need a rewrite. It's not the end of the world. It may be the beginning of your new world.

Let's move on to the fourth zone—the Intimate Zone. In the Intimate Zone you love.

CHAPTER

·7·

A Language Called Love: The Intimate Zone

The Intimate Zone is where love is born. Here is where you find the deepest human communication and connection. The Intimate Zone is where there is the most emotional risk and the greatest opportunity for emotional reward. The Intimate Zone is the center of the Four Life Zones, and yet it is the most difficult of human connections to keep. People are often able to find the Intimate Zone but few are able to stay there.

The most sensitive interactions take place in the Intimate Zone. You are in the Intimate Zone if you are with another person and there is no barrier between the two of you. "What, no barrier?" That's right, and that is just what keeps people from entering the Intimate Zone. People want the benefits of closeness but not the emotional vulnerability. When we are truly intimate we are exposed—and that exposure makes the loving connection possible. Without the risk, without the exposure, there is no intimacy. What are we so afraid of? What is someone going to do to us? The worst that can happen in the Intimate Zone is that someone is going to love us. In the Intimate Zone love is born and exchanged.

You can get over a hurt but you never get over love. Love changes you. In the Intimate Zone your main concerns are to love and be loved with commitment and concern. This includes any interaction where you and another *care* and *love* with responsibility.

The focus in the Intimate Zone is the *feelings* the two of you are sharing with each other. You are concerned with how *what* you do affects another person and vice versa. There is no time constraint. Access is there for those people who are able to give and get love. How do you give love? Is it merely that box of Valentine's Day candy? You give love when you see others as they are. And once you understand and see others as they are, you actively accept them into your life. You get love the same way, when someone else sees, understands, and actively accepts you into his or her life. Loving is the most powerful acknowledgment of another's existence. You don't have to do anything to get and give love except find your way into the Intimate Zone. Once you are in the Intimate Zone, you speak a language called love.

For Shelly this was the zone in which she had the hardest time. She found it difficult to let go and let herself be loved. She needed the rewards of the Intimate Zone but all she felt was resentment that her needs were not being filled. She started creating the right place in the Intimate Zone by learning to speak about her most secret thoughts and desires. It wasn't easy because she was very much afraid of possible rejections.

Intimacy requires your activity and intensity. It requires the best of all the zones—it requires the exploration of the Public Zone, the activity of the Social Zone, and the vulnerability of the Personal Zone—and then, most of all, it requires that you "let go" of judgment and "let in" love. You fail in the Intimate Zone when you always expect it to be romantic, fresh, and new. Intimacy has to do with being close, deep, and familiar. Many people want success in the Intimate Zone and yet they fear opening up. What can happen when you open up so completely? You may discover that the other person can't handle the love. If that happens you haven't lost—you have won, because you took the chance and opened up. Love is the process of opening up and discovering what happens once you do.

Slowly Shelly began to trust herself and to know what she needed. The more she opened up, the more she realized that her fears were paper dragons and wooden monsters. As she challenged what she feared, and her self-esteem increased, she learned that others had the right to reject her and that their rejection was no more than an incident, an opportunity for her to refine her skills. Just like any other athlete, Shelly found that she could learn even when she was unsuccessful.

COACH'S NOTE:

Be careful what you run away from. You might succeed.

Shelly entered the Intimate Zone one night while getting ready for bed. Randy was reading a magazine and the television was off. "Randy, I love you." "I know, dear, and I love you, too." "Randy, I don't mean it that way; I don't mean that I like you, because lots of times I get so mad at you I don't *like* you. I *love* you." "I know, honey." "Randy, right now I know you don't know what I mean. I love you even though you don't know what I am talking about; I love you even though you are insensitive; I love you even though you couldn't cry if I died; I love you even though you often don't love me." "You *do?*" "I do."

Shelly had made her first successful foray into the Intimate Zone. More would come. The Intimate Zone has many different facets, and clients bring them all up at one time or another.

Leslie was twenty-nine, single, and an expert at getting to the Intimate Zone, but that was the only place he felt comfortable. He used to tell me that he was just shy. He got such satisfaction from being in the Intimate Zone that he never wanted any relationship unless it was intimate. He had a hard time in the three other zones because he thought they were gross, insensitive, and meaningless. It took him a while before he discovered that to be truly intimate he had to have access to all the different life zones. Shyness is not so much a personality problem as a lack of skills in the Public, Social, and Personal Zones. A shy person is usually using the wrong rules and behaviors in the right zones. He feels inadequate because he is misperceiving and then reacting to his misperception. Leslie found that to be in sync in the Intimate Zone he had to have the freedom to be in the other life zones as well.

Jane made the mistake of thinking that when she was intimate, those she was intimate with would know what she wanted and what she needed without her telling them. Jane experienced failure in her intimate interactions time and again because she didn't know that to be intimate she had to continue being an adult. She wanted someone to take care of her, to love her, to focus on the *her* rather than the *us*. Intimacy is about the *us*. Two equal adults giving and receiving love.

COACH'S NOTES: INTIMATE ZONE RULES AND REGULATIONS

INTIMATE ZONE: The most important factor for success in the Intimate Zone is that you allow yourself to love and be loved. When you are in the Intimate Zone, you don't let distractions, misunderstandings, or hurt feelings disconnect you. In the Intimate Zone the regulations change for most common feelings and activities.

If you are angry—you are angry about *something* and not at the other *person*.

If you are happy—you *share* your happiness with the other person.

If you are sad—you *stay connected* with the other person.

If you are troubled—you let the other person come close when you most feel like running away.

If you are feeling sexy—you share as passionately as you feel. (This often seems riskier than it really is. Your passion is yours— it becomes sex when the passion is mutual. Remember, a rejection at this point is merely an incident—which can be handled just like any other incident. Just because it is intimate doesn't make it more or less difficult. A rejection in the Intimate Zone only means the timing is not mutual. Respect must be paid to your partner's individual timing and rhythm.)

The key characteristic is a willingness to affect another and to be affected by the other person. You take in what is said and emotionally expressed because you trust the other person's love for you. You no longer need to keep your distance.

Sex: Intimacy is not a sexual issue. Intimacy means you are actively bringing your most open and loving self to the connection with another person. When you are sexual and intimate you have found what the sexual revolution destroyed—feelings. Intimacy and sex are filled with feelings.

Intensity: For some reason people have come to think that intimacy is quiet and careful. On the contrary. Intimacy is full of passion, noise, bumping into, action, and caring. Don't forget to use the same intensity once you are intimate as you did while you were getting there.

COACH'S NOTES:

1. Be careful of the person who has the seduction, satisfaction, and separation syndrome. This person will want to be intimate with you—but for him or her, it is the getting there that is important. Be wise with your intimacy.
2. Intimacy must be sustained by what you do with the other person in the three other zones. Intimacy doesn't remove you from life.
3. Once you are intimate with someone, the creative part of a relationship begins.
4. In the Social Zone you have the intensity of newness, while the Intimate Zone offers the intensity of depth. Don't confuse the two.
5. You don't have to wait for an intimate situation to become intimate. Intimacy is based on the level of exchange and communication you have with another person.

CHAPTER
·8·

The Right Zone
Learning Retest

Let's take some new action to find out what you have learned. Take the Right Place Learning Retest.

For each of the following statements respond with a (P) for Public Zone, (S) for Social Zone, (Pe) for Personal Zone, and (I) for Intimate Zone.

1. You are in the lobby of a New York hotel _____
2. You are in the bedroom of a close friend talking about what is bothering you _____
3. You are driving down the freeway _____
4. You are attending a tennis match _____
5. You are playing in a tennis match _____
6. You are watching a tennis match at home with your family _____
7. You are attending a political rally _____
8. You are at a concert with your favorite date _____
9. You are making love with someone you don't know and can't talk with _____
10. You are sitting by the bedside of your mother and she is deathly ill _____
11. You are riding your bicycle through the park on Sunday _____
12. You are having dinner in a new restaurant with your spouse and you are talking about your marriage _____

13. You are at dinner with a group of friends having a great time_____

14. You are at work and the boss is chewing you out for not meeting a deadline_____

15. You are at work and you are talking to one of your co-workers about how depressed he is_____

16. You are at a family wedding and everyone is having a wonderful time_____

17. You are working with your therapist and you are revealing the most intimate details of your life_____

18. You are at an *est* workshop and someone is crying about having been abused as a child_____

19. You are talking on the phone with your best friend about your worries and hopes_____

20. You are making love and you feel a tremendous wave of love and you say, "I love you"_____

21. You are passing a stranger on the street and she falls and you stop to pick her up; she is crying and you comfort her_____

22. You pass a stranger on the street and he yells at you for bumping into him_____

23. You are in a German beer hall drinking and singing_____

24. You are in a meditation group chanting and meditating_____

25. You are in a taxi having a spirited argument about sports with the driver_____

Answers:

1. (P) The hotel lobby is public. Anyone can go there, although in the more exclusive hotels the public is discouraged entry by the doormen.

2. (Pe) When you and a friend are talking about yourselves in a vulnerable way, you are in the Personal Zone. Don't confuse this with a Social Zone sharing of stories about heartbreaks and childhood dramas.

3. (P) The freeway is a Public Zone. Strange to watch drivers yell and scream at each other, as if what was taking place were personal.

4. (P) This is a Public Zone event. This question has a little trick to it. I didn't indicate whether you were alone or with

someone or whether it was a public court or an exclusive tennis club. These factors could have changed the answer.

5. (S) Playing anything is a Social Zone activity. It is amazing to watch people get angry and accuse each other of cheating or other mischief, when those expressions are inappropriate for the Social Zone.

6. (S) This sounds like a personal activity but really it is social. The family is sharing an activity. Granted it is a passive activity, but it is still the activity that is the dominant focus.

7. (P) This is a public event in the Public Zone. This event is not something you usually share with a particular person but with anyone else who happens to be there.

8. (S) You are creating a Social Zone within a public situation. You are sharing the concert and you feel close to your date. It is not made personal by your sharing thoughts and feelings.

9. (S) This is a Social Zone activity. Granted it may seem personal or intimate, but it is really about sharing the activity of sex. The best you can hope for in this situation is the pure physical pleasure. This is a very common but difficult situation that many people find themselves in. They want to be personal and they wind up having sex. Take it from the coach: sex before personal contact is often dissatisfying.

10. (I) This is an intimate situation. Even if your mother cannot talk, there is the shared experience of love.

11. (P) This is a Public Zone activity. If you were riding with a friend, then it would have been a Social Zone event. Your experience is not restricted to you.

12. (Pe) This is a personal event. The two people are talking and taking risks. It doesn't matter that they are in the restaurant. You can create any of the zones wherever you are, as long as you know what you are doing.

13. (S) This is a Social Zone event. There is no risk in this situation and no vulnerability. The mistake here is thinking that these social friends are personal friends. Social friends are those you have a good time doing things with, not necessarily the people you share your vulnerabilities with.

14. (S) You may feel bad, your feelings may be hurt, but it is still a Social Zone activity. Best to keep it that way. Remember, no matter what the boss says, it isn't personal. He or she is

really talking about your performance. If your boss starts to get personal with you, gently guide the discussion back to performance evaluation. Don't let a boss work out his or her personal problems on you.

15. (Pe) You have made the switch from the activity of work to the sharing of personal revelations. This is different from casually telling your personal stories at work. You have to be very careful with personal revelations at work. Many people make work half social and half personal. When they feel good, they work, and when they feel bad, they don't. That is a mistake. If someone feels bad, or you feel bad, go into the Personal Zone briefly, only to return to the Social Zone. It is not the time or the place for too much vulnerability.

16. (S) This is a social event for the guests. For the bride and groom it is a personal event. We often take social events much too seriously. The purpose of any social event is to bring people together through an activity. Once you have done that, just have a good time.

17. (Pe) Working with a therapist can be a social, personal, or intimate event. This situation is personal. It would be social if you were not revealing yourself.

18. (S) This is a social event. It is about the shared activity of the workshop. There is no person-to-person contact without the activity of the workshop. You can cry, laugh, get angry in the Social Zone and still have it remain social. The Personal Zone requires more commitment and vulnerability with another person.

19. (Pe) This is a personal event, even though you are not in the same room with your friend. What matters is the risk taking and the vulnerability that you and your friend share. You can really "reach out and touch someone" with your feelings over the phone. It is often one of the safest ways to start exploring the Personal Zone.

20. (I) This is an Intimate Zone event. The spontaneous and warm expression of "I love you" signifies the level of connection between the two people. When you say "I love you," recognize that you are bonding deeply with another.

21. (Pe) You are creating a Personal Zone in a public situation. When you make contact person to person, you are in the

Personal Zone. It doesn't have to be a long connection but it becomes personal when you feel it.

22. (P) The angry shouting is not personal. It is inappropriate Public Zone behavior. The man yelling is acting as if the Public Zone were his personal domain. Don't get trapped here by reacting. If you walk away, your rush of anger will pass. If you stay and argue, you have lost control because you are hoping to get a personal resolution to a Public Zone event.

23. (S) This is a Social Zone activity because you are sharing the activity. You are going to feel good when you sing along and take action. If you sit quietly, then you will start getting judgmental and depressed. Remember, activity is the key to success in the Social Zone.

24. (S) This is a Social Zone activity just like tennis playing or beer drinking. While you may value the activity of meditation more than beer drinking, it is still the activity that you share with the other people. The great value of meditation is the effort you put into it. You learn actively to "let go."

25. (P) You and the cab driver are in the Public Zone. Anyone else could be there. And the interaction is going to be over very shortly, and you aren't going to see each other again. Better not take this too personally. Perhaps you are having a good time arguing.

Right Place Learning Retest Results

20–25 correct: YOU KNOW HOW TO IDENTIFY THE RIGHT PLACE. Congratulations. Your next step is to start creating the right place for yourself in more stressful and difficult situations. It is important to go beyond knowing and identifying the right place when it is not stressful—you'll increase your good feelings when you begin putting what you know into action in higher-risk situations. It is through your action that you turn understanding into a life skill.

15–20 correct: YOUR RIGHT-ZONE COMPASS IS BROKEN. If you didn't get all the answers right, don't despair. You didn't flunk. You only learned that you are not too familiar with the four zones. Soon you will know every answer to the test as well as you know your own name. Now it is time to begin to pay attention to the world around you. You are probably stuck inside yourself looking for answers, where you won't find them. Remember, very often what you think is wrong *inside* of you indicates that you don't know how to do something *outside* of you. You may be paying too much attention to your mood or how tired you are instead of focusing on what zone you are in and what you can do to make the most of the situation.

0–15 correct: THE RIGHT WHAT???? Be careful if you wound up here with your score. I'd bet your Nonplayer Attitude has the better of you right now. You are probably thinking that you are stupid or should quit. You didn't flunk. You have an opportunity to learn. Let's work together to help you find out about the world. Don't spend another minute thinking about yourself and how to change. To achieve synchrony you have to learn about the Four Life Zones and how to recognize them. Take a break now and when you resume, take the test again and read the answers carefully. This will clear up any confusion. Remember, the tests in this book are really teaching and practice devices. Use them as if you were an Olympic athlete who practices to sharpen his or her weak points.

Knowing about the zones is vital to your success and happiness. If you don't know what zone you are in, you make mistakes—mistakes you often wind up taking personally. Not knowing how to get into sync can make a healthy personality diminish its self-esteem and create stress and tension. What often happens is that we have incorporated our ignorance about the Four Life Zones into our personalities. It is like the story of the woman who cut both ends off the ham before putting it into the oven. When asked why she did it, she said, "It's the way my mother did it." And when the mother was asked why she did it, she answered, "It's the way my mother did it." And finally, when the aged grandmother was asked why she did it, she said, "It wouldn't fit in the pan." Shelly's conclusion about herself was that she was "a worrier," "guilty," "unable to have a relationship," and "suffering from a mid-life crisis." In fact, she was trying to find synchrony without knowing where to look, what the rules were, or how to act when she finally got there. You now know what it feels like to be in sync—"you at your best." So take your time and practice getting there.

COACH'S NOTES:

---

1. Let yourself take action in the four zones even if others do not respond. It doesn't matter if a particular person does or doesn't respond to you—if you keep taking action you are learning to master the Four Life Zones. Don't let glitches or misconnections stop your progress.
2. To achieve synchrony in each of the zones you have to put yourself in the places where what you want is possible. You don't learn about intimacy by talking to yourself and you don't learn about dating by staying in your apartment and you don't learn about tennis at the bowling alley.
3. You are throwing yourself out of sync if you expect perfection in yourself. Remember, you can't have one person's skill in the Public Zone, and another's skill in the Social Zone, and still another's skill in the Personal and Intimate Zones. Synchrony exists for you when you make the most of the situation you are in.
4. You are putting yourself behind the eight ball when you expect yourself to know how to relate to different people and different situations when you have never learned the rules of those situations.
5. It is not important how you have been, but how you want to be. Let your goals guide you.
6. Change occurs when you become aware of your old behaviors and feelings. It is the lack of awareness that reinforces those old patterns.

Section Three

TAKING CONTROL OF YOUR PERSONALITY

CHAPTER

·9·

You at Your Best:
Putting Yourself into Sync

S ync.
It happens. That moment when time slows down and you are in sync with what you are doing, you feel yourself at your best. When you are in sync your experience changes. You no longer wonder about the future. You're there. You're not depending on others or fate for solutions, because you feel complete in yourself at your personal best. Obstacles that once blocked your progress are hurdles you simply jump over.

Roxanne found sync on Fifth Avenue one spring afternoon. The sun was shining and she felt somehow special. The people she looked at looked back. The colors were clearer, the signs were sharper, and the movements around her made sense. For the first time in years she felt exactly like herself. She wasn't worried or tense.

Warren found sync at his audition for a Broadway musical. When the musical director called out his name, Warren walked onto the stage and started to sing. He wasn't scared, as he had been so many times before. His voice was under his control and he could feel the meaning of the words he was singing.

Sharon found sync while making love with her husband. The night was warm and her caring feelings were intense. When she touched her husband, the touch carried with it a thought and a feeling. The sex was deeper than anything she had ever before experienced. It was so dramatically different from the many other times she had made love.

Barry found sync while struggling with his first novel. His coffee was cold and sitting on a pile of papers. As he typed he started to cry. The large, warm tears flowed down his face. His writer's block was a memory. The words cascaded from his fingertips through his typewriter and onto the page.

Barbara found sync on the tennis court. She was hitting the ball and then the entire game seemed to slow down. Shots she usually had trouble making were going in. Her body was relaxed and moving with grace. She was stroking the ball with accuracy and telling effect.

What had happened to each was the experience of personal synchrony. For Roxanne, Warren, Sharon, and Barry, sync happened under different circumstances. But the experience was very similar. What is sync? *Sync is "you at your best" in the present moment.*

The concept of synchrony will help you to understand not only the feeling of being at your very best, but what it takes to achieve it, and the congruence of elements that underlies that feeling.

What you are doing when you find sync does not matter. What matters is that it is vital to your life, happiness, and health. The experience of "you at your best" can carry you through the roughest of times and lead you to new heights of success. It can transport you out of the deepest despair and depression and it can give you the will to live. Furthermore, you will have experienced and discovered the very source of the energy you need to sustain your life.

To help you find sync I am going to ask you to answer two questions:

QUESTION ONE: How do you find sync?

QUESTION TWO: How do you keep from losing sync once you find it?

By the end of the next three chapters you will find there is no single answer for either of these questions. Instead, we will have developed many answers, with each answer showing us a new and more sophisticated way of finding and keeping sync.

COACH'S NOTE

Don't underestimate yourself. You have already experienced moments of what it feels like to be at your best. Our job is to get you to recall those experiences and shape them into an active and guiding awareness.

I found in coaching that this experience of a person at his or her best was the basis for success and happiness. I knew if I could teach people how to find sync, they would have something very precious. I used to think that it was something like Halley's comet, coming and going periodically. Then I realized that *everyone* had these experiences from earliest childhood through adulthood. What people didn't have were the equipment to recognize and retain the feeling. It took me years to recognize sync and create the tools people could use to find it for themselves. The more I studied the phenomenon of "you at your best," the more I realized just how powerful a learning tool it was.

We know that perception of a reward to come is paramount in persuading a person to change. Since fulfilling one's potential by performing at one's best is as stimulating a reward as one can find, I started teaching clients to recall their peak performances in order to use them as reminders of the feeling of success and to guide them toward future successes.

Great champions feel like champions; they aren't looking for a victory to give them the championship feeling. They already have it. The victory only confirms it. They have the inner reference of what success feels like. Champions base their actions on whether what they are doing enhances, sustains, or diminishes the positive inner reference.

COACH'S EXERCISE

When you have found and use "you at your best," you will notice that you like yourself more. When you don't like yourself you often spend time futilely looking for something or someone to give you the feeling that only "you at your best" can give. The more you look for this special feeling on the outside, the less chance you have of finding it. Once you are at home with this feeling, you will ask yourself: Is what I am doing going to enhance, sustain, or diminish this feeling? Don't try to change what you are doing. Just notice what it does to you. Knowing whether you are moving toward or away from your feeling of "you at your best" gives you control.

Once you have the feeling of performing at your best, your inner compass will tell you when you are headed toward success and when you are distancing yourself from it.

When I asked my most successful clients how they achieved success and underwent so many hardships to get there, they all, without an exception, reported that they always had a peak feeling within that told them that what they were doing was right. Without the internal reference of "you at your best," you are running blind. But when you have this reference point, you have all the human radar you need.

So often people get confused about success because they base their understanding of it on the outcome of what they are doing. They think that when they finally hear the applause, or win the award, or get the congratulations, they will have found success. And so they rush toward the final outcome to get to the external reward. In most cases they miss the real success.

There is a problem with basing success on the acquisition of money, prestige, or plaudits. If your success is based on others' giving you something, then you are dependent on them. No matter how well you do, there will be a time when the applause stops, but knowing how to create the feeling of "you at your best" is like finding the fountain of youth or, like the medieval alchemists, transforming base metals into gold. It is one of the great secrets of life.

The more I studied this experience in the lives of my clients and other successful people, the more I realized that "the best" seemed like the best only because there were so many low points in most people's lives. People feel bad so often that they think of feeling good, doing good, and having a sense of self-confidence, well-being, and self-worth as unusual.

How Do You Find "You at Your Best"?

Since you already have had the experience of "you at your best," it won't be too difficult to find again. You have just forgotten it. "You at your best" has happened to you hundreds of times, occasionally for no more than a split second. You may have found it while making a fleeting connection with someone on the street, or while gazing at a painting in a gallery, or while making a perfect golf swing, or in saying "hello" on the telephone. There are other times when you possessed it for minutes or hours or even days. It could have been while writing a college term paper late at night. Or standing up to your boss. Maybe it was while giving a speech or just talking to one of your children. There are moments of "you at your best" when you are driving your car or hiking down a mountain trail.

COACH'S EXERCISE

Right now, I want you to recall a time when you felt yourself at your best. There may be many different times, but choose one that is strong and fresh in memory. Perhaps when you wrote a beautiful poem, or made love with a special harmony, or completed an important work project. Some think of a moment during a game, others of a moment in conversation. It doesn't have to be the biggest event in your life. Note the space I have left after each of the questions that follow. That space is yours. Use a pencil and write your answer to each of the questions. Then when you progress and reread this section you can update your answers.

What was your experience of "you at your best"?

What did it feel like?

What kind of energy did you have?

What kind of motivation did you have?

What was the body sense you had when you were feeling your best?

What kind of self-control did you have?

What kind of attention and concentration did you have?

Now compare that experience to your usual day-to-day experiences. Are you living from your high points or your valleys? What would happen if you had that peak experience every day, moment by moment to guide you? Think about it. Is it possible? When you can find yourself with an awareness of "you at your best," you will know synchrony.

You can expand upon it by creating new versions of that same experience. You will know when you are using "you at your best" as your new reference because you will have a guiding voice. This voice will be stronger than all your negative thoughts and feelings. It will tell you what to do and how to do it. You will find that you won't be reacting to outside events; instead, you will do what is just right for the situation you are in. It will be very much like having a built-in coach. You'll have to take the actions but your new reference point will be there to guide you.

How Do You Keep the Experience of "You at Your Best" Once You Have Found It?

To retain this experience you will have to take control of your personality. Don't be frightened. It's not as hard as you think. Taking control is considerably simpler than living out of control; for once, you are no longer dominated by outside events or inner reactions. Instead, your response is based on the inner reference of "you at your best."

COACH'S EXERCISE

How do you take control over your personality? Here is an exercise I want you to try now, but more important, I want you to use it for the rest of your life. Ask yourself, "Is what I am doing and how I am doing it *enhancing, sustaining,* or *diminishing* my feeling of me at my best?" If you ask this question—even if you can't answer it definitely—then you will have begun to build your inner compass. Before long you will have that question as a guide for every action that you take. You will be learning.

If you are successful at taking control, it does not mean that you automatically become a heartless automaton. Many artists and writers think that if they get to know themselves they will lose their creative fire. Creativity does not have to arise from a seething cauldron. That might be true for some, but many other creative and successful people know themselves very well and they know how their personalities work. They have control and they use that control to increase their creativity and success and the feeling of being at their best.

COACH'S NOTE

If you don't have control over your personality and your life, then who does?

Shelly had very little control over her personality. If things on the outside went right, she usually felt good. But if things went wrong, she went into a tailspin. If a negative thought popped into her head or a troubling fear or anxiety came up, she was helpless to do anything about it. For example, while working on the biggest project of her career, she had submitted a proposal to a large industrial firm, which could contract with Shelly's company to do all the accounting. If the contract came through, Shelly had a good chance of becoming a vice-president of her company, and that would mean there would be only one other woman more powerful than she in the entire firm. She sent the proposal in on Monday and they told her they would get back to her in two weeks. On Monday of the third week she had begun thinking, "They won't take it." By Wednesday, the thought had become a full-fledged anxiety attack. Shelly's personality was out of her control.

She and I talked about it on Thursday and she was a mess. She wanted to know what I thought the outcome would be. I told her the outcome wouldn't matter at all if her thoughts could do this to her. She had totally forgotten what her best was like. Shelly and I spent the coaching session going over what she felt like at her best. It was very difficult for her to recall it because she kept waiting for the "successful contract" to give her back that feeling. At one point I asked her, "What will it feel like when you hear that you have won the contract?" "I'll feel great." "But I thought you have felt great at other times?" "I have, but this will be different." "Will it?" She stopped and looked at me with a wry smile on her face. "I get it."

What is it that Shelly understood? Just like the rest of us, Shelly has learned to think that how she feels is dependent on what happens *out there.* The truth is if you let the "out there" control how you feel, you are dependent. But when you have control over how you feel, then you can fully enjoy your successes for what they are—successes and not flukes.

COACH'S NOTE

The experience of "you at your best" is your SELF deep within you. When you are experiencing your self, your personality is working at its optimum level. The self is an active awareness, an effortless form of concentration, which you can develop just as you develop any part of your body. The stronger your self becomes, the easier it gets to keep "you at your best" as your reference point for being in sync.

Let me give you another example of the work Shelly did to take control.

SHELLY: I was so mad yesterday I could have screamed.

RICHARD: What happened?

SHELLY: Randy made me so mad by coming home late, when he *knew* we were going to a dinner party. The later he got, the angrier I got.

RICHARD: He made you angry?

SHELLY: Yes, what he did made me angry. O.K. What are you getting at?

RICHARD: It sounds as if you are just some poor kite in the wind. Or do you think there might have been something else you could have done? Some other options you might have had?

SHELLY: Like what?

RICHARD: While you were so busy getting mad, it seems you were forgetting something.

SHELLY: Like?

RICHARD: The party. Were you excited about the party? What happened to the good feelings you had?

SHELLY: I lost the good feelings because of the anger.

RICHARD: Lost?

SHELLY: Lost, like in angry, like I am getting right now with you.

RICHARD: Am I making you angry?

SHELLY: Yes.

RICHARD: That is just the point, Shelly. You get angry without ever finding out if you want to be angry. Was your anger an effective way to connect? And most important, does the anger make you feel good?

SHELLY: No. When he got home I had this urge to greet him and be excited, but before I knew it we were fighting. I wound up having a terrible time at the dinner party and for the next three days.

RICHARD: What would have happened if the anger hadn't gotten out of control?

SHELLY: I would have greeted Randy, and I am sure he would have told me why he was late, and we would have had a great time at the party.

RICHARD: Would you have kept your good feelings?

SHELLY: Yes.

RICHARD: Would you like that option?

SHELLY: Are you kidding? Of course.

For Shelly to find sync meant learning to take control over her personality so that her anger or any other emotion or thought did not control her. Shelly always thought that if she was feeling an emotion, it necessarily dictated her actions. Having an emotion doesn't mean it has to control your personality. When you are angry, you can "have" the anger without becoming an angry person. The same is true for sadness or disappointment. The Spanish language describes emotions better. In Spanish you say, "I have anger." In English you say, "I am angry." *You* are not angry, you are you. You are *feeling* anger. When you start to understand and use this difference, you find yourself much more comfortable with a wider range of emotions—emotions that don't get out of your control. Shelly was just learning how to keep her emotions as emotions and not as directors of her entire life play. Previously, her emotions, her thoughts, and her actions often got out of her control.

Shelly, like everyone else, has moments of control, but real control is being able to use "you at your best" as your inner guide.

In the next chapter you are going to take the Sync Test. This test is another teaching device to help you understand your personality and how it works.

COACH'S NOTE

Remember, by knowing what you need—you strengthen your SELF.

1. When you make the most of each situation you are in, you are preparing the way for your future. And when you don't you

are perpetuating your past. By making the most of each situation, you are learning, growing, and getting everything you can from that situation, and that enables you to do the next thing that comes along.

2. When you are faced with a problem—process the information you possess. How do you process information? Use your brain like a library. Knowledge does not always need to be remembered; you just want to know where it is. Then put what you know into action. Knowledge is not the same as taking action. You want to be able to find and process the information you possess so that you can take action.

3. Whether you feel good or bad, ask "How did I get here? Before I got here, I didn't feel bad (or I didn't feel good) and probably tomorrow I won't be in this mood. I feel this way now—but just for now." This gives you the perspective necessary for action.

4. You don't know what is going on until you are doing the best you can.

5. Opposition is natural. Don't fight opposition. Understand it and move around it. Use it to guide you.

6. In high-level sports, winning is 90 percent attitude and 10 percent talent. You develop attitude through need satisfaction and knowing what zone you are in.

7. Understanding prepares you for action; it does not lead to action.

CHAPTER

·10·

The Sync Test

Take the Sync Test by quickly reading each question and then check yes or no to each. Remember, this is really a coaching device. Take it in order to learn, not to get the right answer.

1. Do you sometimes find yourself so shy that you just can't keep up a conversation? Yes _____ No _____
2. Do you sometimes talk and talk and still find you haven't said what you really meant to say? Yes _____ No _____
3. Do you sometimes think that if you only met the right person your life would change? Yes _____ No _____
4. Do you think that if others understood your position, they would agree with you? Yes _____ No _____
5. Do you sometimes feel like a "victim," that other people are taking advantage of you? Yes _____ No _____
6. Do you sometimes wonder if you are making the right impression on the other people at a dinner party? Yes _____ No _____
7. Do you find that the same things over and over again move you into anger or sadness, anxiety or depression? Yes _____ No _____
8. Do you find that if someone says something to you in the wrong way, you go into a tailspin? Yes _____ No _____
9. Do you have trouble asking for what you want when you want it? Yes _____ No _____

10. Do you have trouble giving yourself permission to have pleasure either in sex or from your successes? Yes _____ No _____

11. Do you sometimes have negative thoughts or emotions that put you down but that you just can't seem to stop? Yes _____ No _____

12. Do you have trouble losing weight, or giving up smoking, or decreasing your drinking? Yes _____ No _____

13. Do you keep picking the wrong people as friends or lovers? Yes _____ No _____

14. Are you afraid to ask for what you want sexually? Yes _____ No _____

15. Do you have secret thoughts you wouldn't tell anyone? Yes _____ No _____

16. Do you find yourself getting angry or resentful at people with authority or successful people who know what they want? Yes _____ No _____

17. Do you forget most of your dreams? Yes _____ No _____

18. Do you get anxious before walking into a party of people you don't know? Yes _____ No _____

19. Do you keep losing friends? Yes _____ No _____

20. Do you get uptight when someone greets you with a hug or a kiss? Yes _____ No _____

21. Do your feelings get easily hurt? Yes _____ No _____

22. If your feelings get hurt, do you find it hard to get over the hurt? Yes _____ No _____

23. Do you find that if someone has hurt you once, you tend never to forget what happened or forgive it? Yes _____ No _____

24. Do you ever notice that you are saying things to impress people without knowing why you do it? Yes _____ No _____

25. Do you find yourself quitting when you feel uncomfortable or when situations get too difficult? Yes _____ No _____

26. Do you notice that you are more comfortable feeling merely O.K. than feeling great? Yes _____ No _____

27. Do you find that if you do feel great, you lose that feeling without understanding why? Yes _____ No _____

28. Do you look for things outside of you to make you feel good? Yes _____ No _____

29. When you feel very good, do you often think, "This can't last"? Yes_____ No_____
30. When you are feeling good, do negative thoughts or disturbing feelings pester you and distract your focus from feeling good? Yes_____ No_____

Total number of yes answers_____

Sync Test Results

0–5 yeses: "YOU AT YOUR BEST." If this is your score, you have a natural ability to find and focus on the inner reference of "you at your best." You aren't waiting for an outside event to bring good feelings. Your inner clock is keeping you right in sync with the best you have. You need to make this inner reference part of your consciousness. Think about it right now. What is the inner reference you are using to guide your life? Begin now to actively use your inner guide. The more you use it, the stronger it will become.

6–12 yeses. YOUR INNER CLOCK ISN'T TELLING THE RIGHT TIME. You know about the right time but you are still not able to stay in the present moment, using "you at your best" as your reference point. You are probably waiting for "you at your best" to occur because of some outside event. That is a common mistake. You know what it means to be at your best but even if you start off with it, you lose it. Or after you are finished, perhaps you have the "flash": I could have done better; I didn't really try. It is hard for you to keep your good feelings at the present moment, but you work hard at finding them. Most likely your reference of "you at your best" needs to get a lot stronger. Don't worry. You just have to develop your sense of good feeling and then you can learn to keep it.

13–30 yeses. YOUR SYNC GAUGE IS IN THE REPAIR SHOP. If you got this many yes answers, you have probably forgotten about "you at your best." Don't worry; you are in good company with most of the world. You can learn how to find sync and be there more often once you learn to use "you at your best" as your new reference point.

When Shelly took this test she answered yes to most of the questions. If she felt good one day, she would lose it the next. And if someone said something to her in the wrong way, she would either get hurt or get mad. She spent much of her time dealing with her reactions—overreactions and underreactions. She didn't have her inner focus of "you at your best." Our next step in her coaching was to teach her how to recall her best and then use it as her daily reference point. But to do that I had to teach her to take control of her personality. The next chapter will tell you what Shelly learned about taking control.

How to Take Control
of Your Personality

Your personality is not, as many seem to think, a mysterious, unfathomable, unmanageable black box. It is an entity you can control and nourish. If you don't, circumstances and other people will be happy to control your personality for you. If you feel bad or good, it's not because of happenstance. It's because of the actions you take or fail to take. An old German aphorism says that God creates an animal, man creates himself. People can re-create their personalities over and over again and increase their effectiveness and good feelings by understanding the dynamics of their personality.

Think about it. Imagine that your personality can be developed just as your body can. It simply requires your decision and follow-up action to perform the exercises. And working with your personality yields far more dramatic results than bodybuilding. Mastering your personality can make you a happy person.

You catch a glimpse of your self through the experience of "you at your best." Your self is not a part of your brain; it is a consciousness born whenever you are "you at your best." The self is the experience of you operating at your actualized potential.

This self can be nurtured into a strong and active awareness that guides your life. There is a great difference between a person who has a strong sense of self and one who doesn't. It has little to do with the quality of performance. It has much to do with how one feels about one's performance. The person who has a strong sense of self feels better about his or her self and creates options, choices, and opportunities.

As your alternatives increase, you are able to adapt more successfully. The self lives with an overwhelming imperative—survival through successful adaptation. To survive, the self creates images or behavior patterns to deal with its circumstances. *The better developed the self, the more effectively will the images (roles) it creates satisfy the imperative of survival through successful adaptation.* When the self is operating at its optimum, it simultaneously adapts to its outer environment and inner needs.

COACH'S NOTE

Let's try to understand the self and its images by comparing them to a tape deck and its cassettes. The self is your tape deck and your images are the tapes. The self is in control of your personality when it plays the right tape (image) at the right time. The images, on the other hand, are limited to what is on the tape. The real problem occurs when you get stuck playing the same tape (image) over and over or playing the wrong tape. This happens when old, out-of-date images are in control of your self.

The single most critical issue anyone must face is the issue of control: whether the self will control the images or the images will control the self. If your self isn't in command, you're living at far less than your potential. The problem is that certain bad images sometimes seem rewarding. The business executive gets rewards for being a workaholic even if it is ruining his or her life, and the mother gets rewards of adulation for being the "perfect" mother. It doesn't matter how much outside praise you are getting from your images—if you are failing to get your needs filled in all four zones.

When your self is in control it creates functional images that satisfy your inner and environmental needs. Images are nonfunctional when they fail to satisfy either of these needs.

When Shelly first started her coaching with me, she had very little sense of her self. She was so busy running from one problem to the next, answering the alarm bells that were going off everywhere, that she had forgotten what she felt like at her best. She was playing the "problem-solving" tape over and over. She had begun to think that she was just a problem solver. She had forgotten her self. I asked her to recall a time when she had felt at her best. It took her ten full minutes and then she was finally able to remember a time when she was on the high-school girls basketball team. There was one particular game in which she was at her best. It was as though she were playing at a different speed. Everything she did went right. Nothing distracted her. This sense of her self was a powerful memory. All we needed to do was harness it and begin using it as her new reference point. I asked her to recall it whenever she was unhappy, having problems, or feeling anxious and then to compare the two ways she could feel. As she learned to do the things that gave her the present-day feeling of self, she was learning to take control. Shelly began to *remember* her self at her best.

COACH'S EXERCISE

Visualize "you at your best." Recall your memory of "you at your best" and then visualize yourself in your present-day situation, but with the attitudes, the emotions and thoughts and behaviors you would have if you were "you at your best." Sense them in your body. You are building the foundation for your success and happiness. Try it. You are going to be surprised.

COACH'S EXERCISE

Recollect a stressful situation in which you forgot "you at your best." Then, next time you feel stress, remind yourself that you are forgetting the new reference of "you at your best." If you feel stress, you're being forgetful. When you are feeling the most stress—then is the time to take a moment and recall "you at your best." That will give you new options, new choices, and an escape from the stress.

I can't emphasize enough that the self is not some vague mystical state. Instead, it is the experience you have already had numerous times in your life, perhaps while hitting a tennis ball, painting a picture, working on a project, playing golf, making love, or driving a car. If the feeling seems distant, you have simply forgotten.

The Parts of the Personality

If the personality resembles the body, then what are the anatomical parts of the personality? Besides the self, there are four major aspects of the personality. There are a survival system, a need system, a reward system, and an image-making system. When these four systems are under control of the self, your personality is operating at its potential. It is growing and getting stronger. I will help you make your entire personality stronger. What you do with it depends on what you want to do with your life. Let's find out about the parts of the personality.

Survival System

Everyone has a survival system and when it is triggered by a real, imaginary, or perceived threat, the body is flooded by neurochemicals that prepare it for "fight or flight."

A lack of control over your survival system indicates that your personality is running amok. You know you've lost control when your fight or flight reaction goes off for reasons other than real do-or-die emergencies. Imagine yourself in a real life-or-death situation. And then imagine yourself in one of your usual imagined life-or-death situations. How often in your present-day life do you react as if you were really in a life-or-death situation, when in fact it is just that your fight or flight reaction has gone off. When that happens you don't have control over your survival system.

Jimmy would fly into a rage whenever the plant manager asked him to work overtime.

Marilyn would get claustrophobia whenever there were too many people in the room.

Bart would find himself avoiding people he knew for fear they would pry into his personal life.

John was a tyrannical boss who browbeat his workers and had a runaway case of high blood pressure.

Whenever Philip felt too much pressure in his marriage, he would go on a three-day drunk.

These people have all lost control over their survival systems. Out of control, the survival system causes havoc in your life. But under your control it becomes a powerful tool for success. Many people don't get control over their survival systems until there is a do-or-die emergency. This is the system people put into action to cram for the big final or to work all night shoring up the swollen river's banks with sandbags. When your survival system kicks into action, your entire nervous system is aroused. Arousal in a controlled state feels good. Successful people have learned to harness their survival systems. They are willing to try new things, take new actions, and stay in intense situations because they aren't frightened when their survival system kicks in. In fact, it feels good to them.

However, when the survival system is in an uncontrolled state, we experience anxiety. Many people who don't have control over their survival systems, and therefore little access to pleasure, will create problems in their lives just to get the "rush" that comes from the arousal of the survival system. Haven't you ever noticed that some people (maybe even you) seem to create mountains out of molehills? It is because of the rush that comes with the created crisis. They are actually getting an inner reward for outer failure. The problem with the survival system is that if you don't know how to use it, you can often panic, have anxiety attacks, or become immobilized because it has been stimulated without your control.

In addition to fight or flight, there is another response the self can add to the survival system—PLEASURE. Pleasure is *controlled arousal.* When you have control over pleasure, you have access to motivation, drive, and the willingness to do what is necessary to succeed. Life is about pleasure—not titillation or superficial turn-ons but the pleasure of being in your body and being in control.

COACH'S NOTE
_____

What would happen if you had 10 percent more pleasure in your life? How would you change? How much less intractable would your problems seem?
_____

If you have control over your pleasure mechanism, you enjoy your life and you are no longer looking for something "out there" to make you feel good.

Before Shelly had control over her survival system she saw crises wherever she turned. If her husband was angry or depressed, or the kids were fighting or crabby, it was a crisis for Shelly. Her system was on emergency alert most of the time and this caused her stress. Scientist Hans Selye warns that with stress there is first an alarm reaction, then the resistance stage, and finally the exhaustion stage. He argues that the ability to deal with stress determines health and happiness.

Shelly was so exhausted emotionally and deprived of the rewards from the four zones that she thought she might "have a nervous breakdown" or "go crazy." As her self took control she was able to break this stress cycle. The self is able to refuse to react and therefore avoid the alarm reaction. But when the self is not in control of the personality, the fight-or-flight part of the survival system runs rampant. Some people create problems, cause delays, and miss deadlines just to activate their survival systems.

Shelly learned to transform the survival system from its focus on life-or-death, do-or-die, fight-or-flight reactions to her own purposes of need satisfaction, growth, and success. The more control she took, the easier it became for her to differentiate between a real crisis that required immediate action and an imaginary crisis.

You create an imaginary crisis when you misperceive a situation and then react to your misperception as if it were real.

For Shelly, this meant discovering that many of the emergencies she was perceiving were the result of being in the wrong life zone at the wrong time. When she was in the Personal Zone with her husband, but using the rules and regulations of the Social Zone, she could sense that something was wrong and she would react with panic. She would wind up fighting and feeling helpless because she didn't know she was in the wrong place at the wrong time.

In coaching we review the false alarms and try to discover new action opportunities. Shelly would tell me about a particularly troubling time and start to have an alarm reaction. Let me give you an example of what we did:

RICHARD: What happened with Randy?

SHELLY: He was so inconsiderate that I got really hurt.

RICHARD: Tell me exactly what happened.

SHELLY: I asked him if he could come upstairs to talk and he said no, he couldn't because he was working.

RICHARD: And then what did you do?

SHELLY: I got hurt and disappointed.

RICHARD: And then what happened?

SHELLY: I got depressed and started thinking we should get a divorce. It took me four hours to get over feeling bad.

RICHARD: Did you satisfy your need to talk to Randy?

SHELLY: No. It is just that I know he is insensitive to me and my needs.

RICHARD: You asked him a question, when it sounds as if you were really telling him you needed to talk to him. He answered your question with an honest but insensitive answer: "No, I am working." But his answer was proof to you that he was insensitive. And that gave you permission to get hurt. What would you have done if you had remembered what you needed?

SHELLY: I would just have told him I wanted him to come upstairs and visit and talk with me.

RICHARD: And what do you think Randy's response would have been?

SHELLY: I think he would have come upstairs.

Shelly and I reviewed scores of her false alarms. Each time she recalled the rush of stress and each time she got better at being able to keep the awareness of "her at her best" and therefore create new action opportunities. She has taken control and no longer has to react just because an emergency bell has gone off. She now knows that each and every moment she has CHOICE.

Most of the stress we experience in our lives is created by our lack of control. When you don't have control you think that what you perceive is reality, rather than simply your perception. And it is your perception that is creating your stresses.

COACH'S NOTES

You create your own stress when you misperceive and you don't know it. You are then reacting to your misperception as if it were the truth.

You have the power to stop your stress reaction by evaluating your perception.

If you are reacting as if it is a do-or-die situation and it isn't, you are being deceived by your perception.

Anger is functional. Either it is a tool to be used to save your life or connect you to someone, or it is occurring because of a misperception.

You must understand your own energy levels. If you are fighting stress, you need recovery time to recharge.

There are stresses outside your control, like natural disasters, but much of the stress in our lives is directly caused by our view of what is happening. It doesn't have to be that way.

COACH'S EXERCISE

Think about any one of your chronic overreactions. Think about just how out of control your survival system is in that situation. And then think about the inner "rush" you get when you do overreact—a rush that no one else knows about. How much of your life have you spent overreacting and then correcting the overreaction? How much choice do you have in those situations?

Taking control is what everyone is trying to do on his or her own without guidance and coaching. If you start monitoring your survival system, you can take control and also have time to start to take control of your need system. The need system is the second part of the personality.

Need System
From birth to death we have needs that continually change. As one need is met another takes its place. And when a need isn't

met, it continues to buzz for attention like a fly on the screen. When your self-awareness is strong and positive, it is able to identify changing needs and activate the survival system to mobilize your personality for satisfying your needs.

In the early part of Shelly's coaching she had very little awareness of what she needed. In fact, when this learning process begins, most people have only the vaguest sense of their needs. Instead they focus on the impulses that keep their images in power. What they ignore are the needs of the self. As Shelly's self became stronger, she got better at identifying her needs. And as her needs were identified, her self was strengthened. She was learning to create a positive growth cycle for her personality. The more you know about your needs, the more quickly you can develop your self. In fact, *needs are such an important part of the personality that I have devoted four entire chapters to them.*

Once you know about your survival system and your needs, the next step is to find out how to use your reward system.

Reward System

The basic rewards of our personal reward system are relief from pain, avoidance of pain, or the feeling of pleasure. These three rewards make up the basic reward system. The first reward is to be able to stop pain. You could be in pain from hunger or cold or loss of love or loneliness or meaninglessness. If the pain becomes great enough, almost any relief is experienced as a large reward. Many people live much of their lives in pain, getting their reward from decreasing it. The second reward is to keep yourself from getting into pain. If you can keep yourself from the pain of hunger, cold, thirst, fear, or whatever, that is rewarding. More common than the relief of pain is the reward of avoiding pain. The problem with this reward is that it keeps you at zero. You can't make any dramatic changes by concentrating on pain avoidance.

Finally, there is the reward that comes from stimulation, newness, growth, and pleasure. These can help you change your life. Studies have been made in which the pleasure centers of rat brains were directly connected to electrical stimulation. The rats could get rewards by pressing a bar, which would then electrically stimulate the pleasure center in the brain. The rats loved it. The rats loved getting the current more than food, sex, or anything else. The appearance of control was a fiction. They were dependent on being in that box. Real control over the reward system means you can get rewards wherever and whenever you want. There are no wires or strings attached. The more control over your personality, the more pleasure rewards you give yourself. As Shelly began to take control over her survival and need systems, her awareness of her self began to get stronger and stronger. The stronger her self became, the more she was able to take control over her reward system.

The reward system is one of the keys to the personality. *You can direct your life because you direct what your rewards are.* When you have control over the reward system, you no longer have to wait for the big success in order to have a reward. You give yourself the reward of recognition and respect for each step you take, for each success you have, and for the effort of trying. One of the most sophisticated rewards you can give yourself is the reward of awareness of what you are doing. After becoming aware, you no longer lose perspective and think that the problem or the crisis is more important than you are.

COACH'S NOTE

It's often hard to teach people how to reward themselves. People are so stingy with rewards, you would think that giving themselves and other people rewards would cause a shortage. There is no shortage of rewards. You don't have to save them up. Start handing them out to yourself and the people in your life.

From childhood on we are taught to surrender our reward system to others. We are taught that the reward of school is an A. Very few teachers have the time to teach the joy of learning. The same is true for much of our present life-style. We are busy merely doing rather than enjoying what we are doing. We can create sync as we learn to reward ourselves with the satisfaction derived from effort and excellence. But we often settle for approval and acceptance. No amount of external approval or acceptance can match internal reward. *The greatest reward is the feeling of the self in control, of being at our best and knowing it.*

For Shelly this meant beginning to do things she wasn't good at in the Four Life Zones. By exploring the unknown in her life she got new rewards from learning new behaviors and taking new risks. Instead of always running back to those things that guaranteed familiar rewards, she was able to get internal rewards by strengthening her self through doing new things.

COACH'S EXERCISE

---

1. Write out the reward system your parents used with you.
2. What reward system do you use today?
3. What reward system do you use with other people?
4. What are the rewards you can get from other people?

As you learn how to use your own reward system and to successfully reward the people in your life, you will find that you are in the right place most of the time.

You know about the survival system, the need system, and the reward system. The final step in taking control of your personality is to take control of the most important of all the parts—the image-making system. When you take control of the image-making system you have within your power the ability to create the right time wherever you are.

Image-Making System
The image-making system is the interface you can use to be "you at your best." When your self is able to identify its needs, activate the survival system, and coordinate the reward system, it then has the three factors it needs to create new and successful images to satisfy your present-day adult needs. New images are the way the self satisfies its needs, collects rewards, and grows stronger. It is a method of directly increasing your self-confidence and self-esteem, self-worth and self-love. Knowing about the Four Life Zones is important—but they represent the map and not the vehicle. Your images are the vehicles for making the Four Life Zones work for you. *Images are how you interact with the world.*

Images are the acts, roles, or parts you play in life to fill your needs. You already have many images or tapes. Your images are the by-product of the self's adaptation to a particular need at a particular time in a particular place. The image you developed in high school for relating to authorities won't work on the job today. Nor will the image you created in second grade work as you explore the world as an adult. The image your self created to get you food when you lived in an igloo in Alaska won't work in Paris.

There are many problems with our images. The self (or tape deck) that created the image (tape) was different from today's self. Our needs were different before and the situation we were in was different. Needs, environments, and self change—images don't. Images are merely memory patterns that react to certain stimulation. Whether we like to admit it or not, parts of our personalities react just like Pavlov's dogs. Advertisers seek out the signals or buttons that will get us to respond to their ads regardless of whether we need their products or not. Just think about all the different images you have stored in your memory, ready to kick into action when a certain button is pushed. What are some of your buttons—work, sex, anger, being right, being perfect? *Images are such an important part of the personality that I have written three chapters just about them.*

You now have a general working knowledge about the parts of your personality machine. When you learn to get the parts working in harmony, you can get your personality running like a fine racing car. Let's go on to the next chapter, where we are going to find out about more needs than you ever knew you had. Remember, by knowing what you need—you strengthen your self.

COACH'S NOTES

1. When you make the most of each situation, you are preparing the way for your future. And when you don't, you are perpetuating your past. By making the most of each situation, you are learning, growing, and getting everything you can from that situation, and that enables you to do the next thing that comes along.

2. You can break panic by taking a single, small action—now, when it counts.

3. Despair is the realization that you don't have control. Despair is countered through consistent action. Control comes with consistency.

4. Anxiety is a function of passivity. The more you sit and do nothing the more anxious you become. Anxiety is withheld energy.

5. Anger can be controlled by the self or its images. If it is controlled by the self, then it connects or protects. If your anger is controlled by your images, then it punishes and disconnects.

6. Rewards should be based on the feeling you already possess. Ask yourself, "Is what I am doing going to enhance, sustain, or diminish my good feeling?"

7. High external intensity becomes pressure when there is no internal intensity to match it. If you fear high intensity you need to increase your inner intensity. Intensity is relative.

8. When you are faced with a problem, process the information you possess. How do you process information? Use your brain just like a library. Knowledge does not have to be remembered; you merely want to know where it is. But knowledge is not action. You want to be able to find and process the information you possess so that you can take action. Processing information breaks unproductive patterns.

9. Irrational and nonsatisfying behavior makes sense only within the context of misperception.

10. The self has the power to evaluate perceptions and therefore to control reactions to perceptions. How do I know I am misperceiving? If I don't have options.

Section Four

NEEDS–
THE
PERSONALITY
FUEL

·12·

Self-confidence

Wouldn't it be wonderful if you could increase your self-confidence, self-esteem, self-worth, and self-love? In the next four chapters that is exactly what you are going to learn to do. In the last section we learned about the personality and started to consider taking control of it. In the next four chapters you are actually going to take control. How? You have to tell your personality what to do. Remember that the personality is a need-satisfying machine. If you can speak to your personality in terms of needs, it automatically and consistently responds. Once you tell your personality what you need, it is set in motion. But if you don't know what you need, your personality becomes susceptible to the commands of your images, which can make you miserable.

For so very long people have believed that these self-enhancing qualities of self-confidence, self-esteem, self-worth, and self-love developed in childhood and carried over from there. If you had them as a child, then you had them as an adult. But what you get from your childhood is only the beginning of the game. It is not the final score. You can have a terrible childhood and still develop the self-enhancing qualities later on. The secret is learning about your needs in the different zones.

When you have self-confidence you are willing to take new chances and try new things. As your self-esteem grows, you risk placing yourself near the people you want to be with, and as your self-worth grows you send out signals that you are to be treated with respect. When your self-love is high, you let people love you and you let yourself love.

What You Get from Each Zone

SELF-CONFIDENCE: You create self-confidence when you learn how to fill your Public Zone needs.

SELF-ESTEEM: You create a higher self-esteem by filling your Social Zone needs.

SELF-WORTH: You create more self-worth when you feel Personal Zone needs in yourself and others.

SELF-LOVE: You create more self-love by satisfying your Intimate Zone needs.

Let's do this exercise to get moving in a positive direction.

COACH'S EXERCISE

Think about how your life would change:
If you had more self-confidence in the Public Zone.
If you had more self-esteem in the Social Zone.
If you had more self-worth in the Personal Zone.
If you had more self-love in the Intimate Zone.
Once you have thought about how your life would change, visualize a situation for each of the four zones and how you would be different with more self-confidence, self-esteem, self-worth, and self-love.
Rehearse it in your mind.
Feel it. What would it feel like?
When you add up the four new ways, you are at your best.

Increasing Your Self-confidence

People who seem naturally self-confident have an advantage in the high threshold of their survival-system alarm. It doesn't ring for false alarms. They don't overreact. They take calculated risks that can enrich their lives and never seem overwhelmed by their environment. To a great extent, self-confidence is a *function* of satisfying Public Zone needs.

You can be confident in a desert if you have enough water to drink and a compass to guide you to an oasis. But without water or a compass, the desert might terrify you. The same is true in the Public Zone, where satisfactions give you a sense of competence in the real world. On the other hand, if you don't know how to fill your Public Zone needs, you start barking up the wrong trees in your quest for contentment. And the more deprived you are, the less confident you become.

I'm sure it's happened to you. Those days when you were outside, just walking, when strangers seemed friendlier and the whole world seemed exciting and inviting. At other times, that same world seemed frightening and strangers seemed brusque and unfriendly. But guess what? It wasn't the world that had changed; it was you. What was the difference? When you felt good, you were satisfied and confident, and when you didn't feel good, it was because you were lacking satisfaction.

Let me show you how people can increase their self-confidence by learning to satisfy their Public Zone needs. Here is an example.

Kenny is a twenty-five-year-old client of mine who was a total stranger in the Public Zone. By the time he was twenty-four he had tried to kill himself three times, was a confirmed alcoholic, and was chronically depressed. It was no wonder. His life was a modern-day Charles Dickens story. He had an abusive father who never rewarded him for anything he did well and punished him for anything he did less than perfectly. Unable to be perfect, Kenny quit trying. He stopped caring, stopped feeling. He was even unsure of what he liked and did not like. New people and new situations scared him.

Kenny's mother was passive and withdrawn when the father was around but very charming and warm when he was gone. By the age of twelve Kenny was more interested in boys than girls, but he found it much easier to be with girls because of their sensitivity. He had his first homosexual experience at fifteen with a man of nineteen. Kenny didn't like himself very much. He came to me while he was breaking up with his boyfriend of four years and he was terribly depressed.

Like many people, Kenny didn't know what he needed because he had been deprived for so long. He thought he was a failure. He didn't have the self-confidence, the self-esteem, the self-worth, and the self-love that come from knowing how to identify and satisfy needs.

To get Kenny started, we focused first on his Public Zone needs.

COACH'S NOTE

When you don't know what you need, you try to solve problems to get satisfaction. You don't realize that problems occur because you aren't satisfying your needs. When you satisfy your needs, your problems decrease.

First I got Kenny to start thinking about his needs in the Public Zone. Once you know what you need, your entire personality seeks new opportunities to fill the needs you have identified. How many people do you know who have lived for years on a starvation diet as far as their needs are concerned? What about you? What needs do you let yourself know about? Take this test and find out about your Public Zone needs.

The Public Zone Needs Learning Test

The needs test is a teaching device. For each need described, give yourself a 1 if the need is filled, a 0 if the need is not, and a −1 if you have never even thought about the need. As in all the surveys and tests in the book, these needs represent only some of the needs you may have. Not all needs pertain to each of the four zones. Think about all of the different Public Zone needs questions so that you can stimulate your awareness.

___1. **The Need for Safety:** You need to feel free to explore the Public Zone and go where you please. You are unafraid of traveling or of being with strangers.

___2. **The Need for Excitement:** You need to do new things and different things so that you aren't falling into the same rut each day, doing the same things, thinking the same thoughts, and feeling the same emotions. You expose yourself to new perspectives.

_____**3. The Need for Exploration:** You need consciously to break your own patterns of travel, communication, and use of space. It means you literally move your body through the world in different ways.

_____**4. The Need for Freedom:** You need both internal and external freedom. You are not restricted through your own fears or someone else's control.

_____**5. The Need for Information:** You need to know what is happening in the world, where things are, what is new and exciting, the places and people you might wish to explore. It is like knowing how to use the public library, with the entire Public Zone as your card catalog and reference shelf.

_____**6. The Need for Access:** You need modes of transportation to get places, just as you need information media to learn. These are a vital Public Zone need.

_____**7. The Need for Citizenship:** You need to have a country that is your country, a city that is your city, a territory that is your area. It means you have public rights in these places.

_____**8. The Need for Skill:** You need to know and to be adept at getting information, making contact with other people, knowing how to behave in the Public Zone.

_____**9. The Need for Flirtation:** You need to know that you're attractive and to compliment others on their attractiveness. It means letting other people know you are there. It is not so much sexual as it is a need for acceptance from members of both sexes.

_____**10. The Need for Intelligence:** You need "street smarts" and the "social smarts" of knowing what areas, what times, what people to get to know and whom and what to avoid.

Total Public Zone Score_____

Public Zone Needs Learning Test Results

5–10: SELF-CONFIDENT. Congratulations. You are filling your Public Zone needs and you have a good sense of how the Public Zone works. If you spend a little more energy learning about your Public Zone needs, you can maximize your self-confidence. The more self-confident you become, the more you can develop the ability to teach others how to have a good time in the Public Zone. Next, focus on those situations in the Public Zone in which you overreact. Your overreactions are the result of trying to get more from the Public Zone than is possible. Use your self-confidence to explore new areas in the Public Zone. Study all the different happenings, the different people, and then put yourself in those new situations. Remember, the more time you spend in the Public Zone, the more assets you will have to bring to your other relationships.

0–5: CONFIDENT??? If this is your score, you may frequently feel uncertain and uncomfortable in the Public Zone. You probably know what you would like to be, but don't know how to get there. Take heart. You are in a position to do something. Look for opportunities in the Public Zone to do something new. Remember, you have got to spend time in the Public Zone if you want to become comfortable there.

−11–0: SHY. Welcome to the club. So many people are shy with strangers. You are just shy most of the time. Shyness isn't a disease or character fault—it is just a sensitivity gotten out of hand. You can take control by learning the Public Zone rules and regulations. You may be shy because you don't know how easily you can find satisfaction in the Public Zone. That is probably because you are trying to fill personal and intimate needs there. You want the Public Zone to be friendlier and more comfortable than it is. The Public Zone is there for your stimulation and excitement. Use your sensitivity to draw you into this zone and heighten your pleasure.

You can get a tremendous boost in your self-confidence by learning to identify your Public Zone needs. You probably think that because you are shy, there is something wrong with you. There isn't. You are just turned in the wrong direction—inward. The Public Zone is *out there* with all those people you don't know; it is not inside you. In the Public Zone you don't need to think about yourself; you need to interact with all those strangers *out there.*

I started Kenny's coaching in the Public Zone because he took this test and found himself in the "Shy" scoring range. He was not sure of himself in the Public Zone. You might ask, why start in the Public Zone? It is because the real world begins out there in the Public Zone and it's the zone of least risk.

We walked together a lot. His homework? To get out of the house, to smile at people, to learn what was happening on the outside. This was really difficult for Kenny, because he felt like a stranger everywhere he went. The paradox of change is that if you want to be successful, you have to do the things you are not good at; you have to do the things that frighten you. That doesn't mean that you have to hang-glide or do an Evel Knievel rocket act across the Grand Canyon. It means you have to stop, think, analyze what you have to do, break it down into do-able steps, and then take the first step. It took Kenny four months to start feeling comfortable in the Public Zone, but in the process he gained something he hadn't known before: self-confidence. His new confidence gave him more to say when he was in the other zones and he wasn't nearly as shy.

COACH'S NOTE

All those other people in the Public Zone really aren't looking at you and they don't care what you're doing. And if they do, *they* are in the wrong zone. Relax, the Public Zone is like an admission-free Disneyland.

One of my clients used to be terribly afraid of the Public Zone. Diane lived in New York City on the Lower East Side, parts of which are, well, rough. She could afford no better place to live. For her the Public Zone seemed like a formidable place. She used to be afraid of meeting strangers. But on the other hand, she was bored with many of the people she knew. She kept telling herself that she was too shy, that she couldn't do it, or that other people were too scary, or as a last resort, that if she met new people, they would all be the same. The truth of the matter was that she didn't know what she needed in the Public Zone. She was confused. Whenever she thought of needing anything, she thought about her most personal and intimate needs. And no matter how hard she tried she was never going to fill her personal and intimate needs in the Public Zone. No one does. But it's a start to improving your relationships in the other zones.

To get Diane to find herself at her best we had to start with what she needed in the Public Zone. Diane learned that she needed to be outgoing, assertive, outspoken, and inquisitive in the Public Zone. She started filling those needs by taking little steps.

One day she totally surprised herself. She was walking down her neighborhood street and she saw four hoodlums pick a woman's purse. Diane walked past and then turned and started to shout in her loudest voice, "Lady, those men just took your wallet." The woman turned and started to shout. Other people turned and several men surrounded the thieves.

Bottom line: The woman got her purse back and Diane walked with her head higher. She had found the self-confidence she was looking for. She wasn't so shy after all. Before long Diane started up conversations with strangers and discovered that there was an entire world of people out there. Many of them were just like her—lonely but willing to make a friendly connection. She discovered that her worst fears were unfounded. The hard part for her was learning to let people pay positive attention to her. The more outgoing she became, the more people would smile at her, pay her compliments, and talk to her. She was no longer trapped by needs she didn't know about.

Many people come to seek counseling in order to become independent of the world—to become so rich, so successful, and so separate that they won't ever need anything again that they can't get from themselves. They're headed in the wrong direction. Don't abandon this beautiful world. Learn how to appreciate its surprises and variety and excitement. Live in it as it is.

Needs are not something to be avoided but something to be cultivated. Needing does not mean you immediately get what you want, but the moment you allow yourself to know what you need you are on your way toward "you at your best."

The most deprived people I know are those who do not know what they need. They are unhappy because they continually settle for what is available when an opportunity finally surfaces into awareness. You fall in love with the person who waited on you at the shoe store or you think that taking abuse will eventually lead to true love. I hear the same thing time and again from clients—how they suffer until suddenly they seem to break free by grabbing on to some person, some idea, or some thing. Then before long, they realize they have made another mistake. The more you know about your needs, the less you have to wait for that right person or right situation to come by to give you satisfaction.

Learning about your needs is like finding a vaccine against depression and worthlessness. What is possible is nothing less than a life with you in control over yourself.

In the next chapter we learn about your Social Zone needs.

Self-esteem

S elf-esteem gives you good feelings, power, and as-
surance. Without self-esteem, ants become rhinos and
the curb seems too high to step over. Many people believe that if
they had more power, higher status, less weight, they would have
more self-esteem. You don't have to wait for self-esteem. You can
create it by learning to satisfy your Social Zone needs.

With self-esteem there's nothing to hold you back from playing
the game of life, from taking a chance, from following through in
playing your roles. You may not always take star billing. That's
not the point. The point is, with self-esteem you're playing the
game and you have the opportunity to win and the right to lose.

Think about it. You increase your self-esteem when you care
about yourself. You express care when you know how to identify
what you need and can fill those needs. What Social Zone needs
do you let yourself know about? Take this test to get yourself
started toward more self-esteem.

The Social Zone Needs Learning Test

The Social Zone needs test is not a test to pass; it is a test to
learn from. For each need described, give yourself a 1 if the need
is filled, a 0 if the need is not filled, and a −1 if you have never
even thought about the need. These, of course, are only a representative sampling of Social Zone needs. (As are the other surveys and tests in this book.)

_____**1. The Need for Activity.** This is the need to do things: work, play, socialize, almost anything. The essential feature is the doing with other people. It means that you don't let depression or inconvenience stop you from taking action and doing things with other people.

_____**2. The Need for Success.** You need to know how to succeed in the Social Zone. For each activity there are inner and outer success criteria. To meet your outer criteria you need recognition by others that you are doing well, and to meet your inner criteria you yourself have to acknowledge when you do well. To satisfy the need for success, both criteria require fulfillment.

_____**3. The Need for Competence.** You need to know how to do things well in the Social Zone. This means knowing how to meet your Social Zone needs through activities. When you are competent in the Social Zone, you recognize the competence of others. You don't have to come out on top everywhere.

_____**4. The Need for Performance.** You need to perform whatever you are doing the best you can. This means feeling yourself taking action. You are establishing your place in the world through your actions.

_____**5. The Need for Participation.** In the Social Zone, whatever you do, you do *with* somebody else. There are times when you do things alone in the Social Zone, but the need for participation generally requires your connection with another person.

_____**6. The Need for Respect.** You need to be respected for what you do and how you do it. This means that the activity you are doing is important to you and to those with whom you do it.

_____**7. The Need for a Group.** You need to have peers for different Social Zone activities. There are work peers, sports peers, and social peers. The need for a social group in which you are accepted as one of the crowd is important.

_____**8. The Need for Fun.** You need to experience joy, humor, and lightheartedness. To get these things you have to relax your defenses.

_____**9. The Need for Health.** You need to be free of major illness and drug and alcohol problems.

_____ **10. The Need for Sex.** You need to have sex just for the pleasure of the activity.

_____**11. The Need for Sports and Exercise.** You need to have a regular program of exercise and sports, which allows you to develop your kinesthetic or body intelligence.

Total Social Zone Score_____

Social Zone Needs Learning Test Results

5–12: SELF-ESTEEM. You have it. You have enough satisfaction in the Social Zone to have a strong sense of self-esteem. You can now take two new steps. First: Focus on those needs that aren't being filled. Create a new list of Social Zone needs to increase your self-esteem even more. Second: Focus on the Social Zone needs of other people. If you are getting your Social Zone needs met, take the time to understand the Social Zone needs of the people you are with.

0–5: WORRIED BUT WILLING. So many of us get caught here. We know what we want to do in the Social Zone but we spend too much time worrying about it. In the Social Zone there is no reason to worry—this is the "take action" zone. Once you have taken the best action you can at that moment—forget it. Worrying keeps you from knowing what new social needs you can fill. You probably spend as much time wondering about what to do and when to do it as you do taking action.

　　You can do something dramatic and stop living on starvation rations. First, identify your needs. Then take control of your images and focus on the enjoyment that comes from taking action. Your score suggests that you are trying to fill needs in the Social Zone that probably arise from the Personal and Intimate Zones. Stick to the Social Zone needs in the Social Zone.

–11–0: DOWN BUT NOT OUT. *Been Down So Long It Looks Like Up to Me* is the title of a book, but it is probably your motto if you scored this low. You are spending too much of your time being fearful. Let's do something about it right now. If you scored between –11 and 0 you can simply take some new actions to produce visible results. How? Review the Social Zone needs list. What are your needs? Think of a new action opportunity that would fill each of those needs. Then just incubate it. You don't have to do anything. Your self will get stronger just by knowing that it is all right to need. And before you know it, you will have created new images to satisfy your needs.

One of my clients was really confused about the Social Zone. Jennifer was a middle-aged, unmarried social worker and she had come to the conclusion that she was never going to meet the kind of men she wanted to meet. She kept focusing on what she *wasn't* getting. I taught her to focus on her Social Zone needs and to do something about them. She found she had a need to be assertive and feminine, outgoing and friendly. The more she knew about her needs, the more control she took over satisfying them. She no longer had to be the most beautiful woman in the world, or have the figure of Bo Derek, or be seductive. She stopped waiting for men to appear out of the blue. She found that many men were just as scared, intimidated, and ill-at-ease in the Social Zone as most of the women she knew. Men, too, frequently didn't know what they needed. She didn't have to wait for them to come to her. She started taking the action that worked for her need satisfaction. The basic law of physics was at work: The more action Jennifer took, the more reactions she got from men. She became like a magnet, attracting attention.

If you feel ready, let's go on to the Personal Zone needs in the next chapter.

CHAPTER
·14·

Self-worth

Depression may be the most common psychological problem people face today. Nearly everyone will undergo some form of depression in his or her lifetime. For many it will be a life-disturbing experience; for others it will take away the joy of being alive.

Far worse than depression is a loss of self-worth. If you have self-worth, a temporary stress overload that produces depression can be managed. But without self-worth, very little makes sense. The feeling of self-worth enables you to appreciate yourself and others no matter what is happening. And yet, when people face depression, they try to overcome the depression rather than increase their self-worth—but it is often a deficiency of self-worth that makes one susceptible to depression in the first place. I see people who are generally successful in the Social Zone and yet, if they don't know how to make those Personal Zone connections that satisfy their needs, often experience a loss of self-worth. And a decline in self-worth is just one step removed from depression. You can increase your self-worth by learning about your Personal Zone needs.

Knowing about your Personal Zone needs and how to fill them is important. It protects you against depression and keeps you in touch with yourself. You don't react to every stress as if it were do-or-die. Self-worth is like a sea anchor—the stronger your self-worth, the more secure you are in any of life's storms. You feel more capable of venturing out and risking more emotionally and intellectually.

COACH'S NOTE

As I have mentioned so often: *When you don't know what you need, you often try to solve problems to achieve satisfaction.* You don't realize that problems occur because you aren't satisfying your needs. When you satisfy your needs your problems decrease.

The Personal Zone Needs Learning Test

For each need described, give yourself a 1 if the need is filled, a 0 if the need is not filled, and a −1 if you have never even thought about the need. Again, as elsewhere in this book, I am mentioning only a representative sampling of needs.

_____**1. The Need for Closeness.** This is the need for personal interaction. It means knowing you care about someone and someone cares about you. This caring is not related to what you do or to your status.

_____**2. The Need for Sharing.** You need to be able to share what you think and feel without judgment. This requires skills to express yourself and to listen.

_____**3. The Need for Growth.** You need to know that you can change and that you are not stuck where you are. This is the need for stimulation and excitement based on knowing how your personality operates and how the personalities of others operate.

_____**4. The Need for Self-knowledge.** You need to know what you feel and why, what you dream and what your dreams mean, what you fear and why, what you desire, what your goals are and how to get there, how your mind works and how to control it. This means having insight into your own life.

_____**5. The Need for Feelings.** You need to know the difference between your feelings and your emotions. Emotions are those reactions that resemble neurochemical storms over which you may or may not have much control, while feelings give you basic awareness of your sensations, your body energy, and your sexual pleasure. Both make it possible for you to cry, to get angry, to be joyous. They reflect a strong life energy.

_____**6. The Need for Pleasure.** You need to know the most fundamental reward of being alive. It is having direct access to what gives you the good feelings about being alive.

_____**7. The Need for Caring.** You need support, concern, stroking, understanding, and the motivation that comes from receiving affection from others.

_____**8. The Need for Caring for Others.** You need to give concern, strokes, understanding, and motivation to others.

_____**9. The Need for Friends.** You need people in the Personal Zone who know what it means to be friends, people whom you trust and who trust you. You need friends of the same sex and friends of the opposite sex.

_____**10. The Need for Sex.** You need sexual pleasure derived from letting yourself enjoy completely your own and someone else's affection and desire.

_____**11. The Need for Mutual Respect.** You need to give and get respect. This means that there is no calculation of special status or social hierarchy. It means you are able to sense the self of another person and he or she can sense your self.

_____**12. The Need for Equality.** You need to be able to stand side by side with someone you care deeply about and know you are equal.

Total Personal Zone Score_____

Personal Zone Needs Learning Test Results

5–12: SELF-WORTH. It feels good to know that you are worth something to yourself and others. What we want to do now is to build on it. If you are satisfied in the Personal Zone, then you have the resources to increase your self-worth. Self-worth can be built directly upon your ability to satisfy your needs. Find out the ways and situations in which you lose your good feelings. *Do you blow up and get angry after things get too good? Do you lose your cool when things get too negative or intense?* Focus on taking control of a single overreaction situation. You will be pleased with the results.

0–7: ALMOST THERE. You are on the edge between self-worth and worthlessness. You are breaking even in the Personal Zone, getting just enough need satisfaction to give you a long-term case of despair. It is time to start changing. You don't want to let your Personal Zone needs go unfilled too long. To change you have to challenge your images so that you can start to learn what your Personal Zone needs are. Most often it is one's out-of-date images that keep one from knowing what one needs.

–12–0: NEEDS A SELF-WORTH CHARGE. You need some Personal Zone coaching. If you fit into this category, you probably feel worthless fairly often. I have felt worthless at different times in my life, and it is one of the most painful of experiences. But I have found that something can be done about it. Sit back right now and take a breath and listen to me for a minute: You are worth all the good that life has to offer. It is just that your images are not working for you and they are therefore robbing you of the essentials you need for self-esteem and self-confidence and, most of all, self-worth. You can take two steps right away—study the Personal Zone needs and then start reviewing your images and how they function in the Personal Zone. Once you know what is wrong, you can stop reinforcing your old behaviors through unconscious repetition. These two steps are like an emergency field dressing on a war wound. We want to stop the psychological blood loss from your out-of-date images. When you do this exercise, you will notice that you will start feeling better, and once you feel better, you can focus on filling more of your Personal Zone needs.

Personal Zone needs are often confusing to identify. One of my clients kept complaining of loneliness. And yet we couldn't discover what needs were not being satisfied. He had friends; he was married and had a child. But still he was lonely. He and I discussed his Personal Zone needs in more detail and we found a need that was totally unfilled. He had a need for a male friend, someone with whom he could talk man to man. It was not that his wife was lacking something. It was a quality Abraham needed from another man. Once he discovered what he needed, he learned to develop the kind of friendships that he'd been missing since childhood. We developed a strategy for him to start finding those other men he needed in his life. At first it was difficult because Abraham would react to the miscues and lack of closeness as a sign that the friendship wasn't working out. He learned to be persistent and in the end he developed three close male friends within a year's time. To develop the friendships required that he spend time in the Personal Zone, take personal risks, and expose his vulnerable side. As he did, his self-worth increased. The more you risk, the greater your self-worth becomes.

Let's go on to the Intimate Zone Needs Learning Test and find out about love and intimacy.

CHAPTER

·15·

Self-love

Have you ever had your heart broken? I don't know
anyone who hasn't. There is something special about
a heartbreak because it opens us to our most intimate needs.
When we make an intimate connection with another person,
there is the possibility that we are going to have our deepest
needs filled. And when that doesn't work out, we find ourselves
heartbroken. There is no quicker way to set yourself up for a
heartbreak than to start a relationship and not recognize your
intimate needs. Recognizing your intimate needs is a key to
knowing how to find the right place in your relationships. Narcissism is a failed attempt at self-love, and while psychologists and
sociologists report on the horrors of narcissism, they find it much
harder to teach us how to love ourselves. And if there is anything
that you need to live your life, it is self-love. Self-love is a quality
that can be nurtured and enhanced through satisfying your Intimate Zone needs.

The Intimate Zone Needs Learning Test

The Intimate Zone needs test is another test about loving yourself. It is difficult to love yourself when your intimate needs
aren't being met. For each intimate need described, give yourself
a 1 if the need is filled, a 0 if the need is not filled, and a −1 if
you have never even thought about the need.

_____**1. The Need for Love.** You need to be connected to another person and have that special feeling of contact, bond, and attachment.

_____**2. The Need for Understanding.** You need to understand yourself and have someone else understand you. This means you and someone else have taken the time to get to know each other so as to interact more deeply.

_____**3. The Need for Truth.** You need to tell the truth and hear it from someone who cares about you. This is a loving truth that supports and builds no matter how painful it may be when you first hear it.

_____**4. The Need for Altruism.** You need to do for others out of the goodness of your own heart. You need to care about the welfare of another without seeking reward.

_____**5. The Need for Bonding.** You need to connect with another adult in those moments when you totally let down your defenses.

_____**6. The Need for Spiritual Understanding.** You need to have experiences and to explore the complex nature of the universe and man's place in it.

_____**7. The Need for Sex.** You need a loving and totally free sexual relationship where the medium of exchange is sexual love.

Total Intimate Zone Score_____

Intimate Zone Needs Learning Test Results

4–7: SELF LOVE. You are one of the few. You have self-love. It is time for you to take this power to love yourself and spread it around. I am asking you to do something difficult—to love others even when they can't love themselves. Take a chance on filling all your intimate needs, and your self-love will become a guide and inner reference for you. You will perceive when this is right for you and when it is not.

0–3: LOVABLE. You are lovable . . . but waiting to get started with real self-love. Let's start right now. Get ready for a big dose of self-love, if you are willing to take the time and effort to find out what your Intimate Zone needs are. This love will be based on satisfaction and caring for yourself and others. If you scored 0–3 it means your images are as much a source of trouble as they are of rewards. Think about images you use in the Intimate Zone that decrease your self-love. Then focus on those images that would enhance your self-love by filling your intimate needs.

−7–0: HEARTBROKEN. No one can break our hearts quite as well as we can break our own. You have a broken heart because your intimate needs aren't being filled. You aren't alone. You can do something new. Many people have problems in the Intimate Zone. If you scored in the "Heartbroken" category it is time to admit you are ready for lots of new satisfaction. What images would help you satisfy your intimate needs? Visualize what they are and how your life would change if you were in control of them. What is your best image in the Intimate Zone? Use that feeling to guide you.

Bart was an interesting client. He was thirty-six and had many lovers but no truly intimate ones. He had traded being gay for going asexual as a result of a lack of intimacy. Bart was able to blend masculine strength with sensitivity and yet he was caught in a life-style that excluded intimacy. He had become despondent because he had abandoned his needs for intimacy. Now he learned that these needs were far more important than he had ever realized. Bart and I worked on his Intimate Zone needs and he learned not to settle for physical contact when what he wanted was emotional nourishment. He found there were other gay men just like him who wanted intimacy and love. He wasn't trying to hide his needs from himself any longer.

How to Like Yourself

We have just spent four chapters learning how to like ourselves. As simple as it seems, you like yourself when you fill your needs. In the Public Zone you like yourself when you take action, when you present yourself in a friendly and dynamic way. You like yourself in the Social Zone when you are performing at your best. You like yourself in the Personal Zone when you allow yourself to be vulnerable and experience "you as you are." And finally you like yourself in the Intimate Zone when you love yourself. You love yourself by learning to accept yourself as you are and by accepting others as they are. Liking yourself isn't dependent on what anyone else thinks but on your own valuation of yourself. You can't prove yourself to anyone else; you can prove yourself only to yourself—and that proof already exists. You are what you have. When you don't fill your personal needs or when you continually make personal responses in social situations, you become confused and stop liking yourself. Liking yourself means you are successfully surviving. Understand what you need and you will learn to go beyond survival to growth and adult development.

Let's go to the next chapter where we learn about the right image. Images are the tools your personality uses to go out into the world to find out how to satisfy your needs.

Section Five

IMAGES:
THE TOOLS OF THE
PERSONALITY

CHAPTER
·16·

The Single Most
Critical Question

W e all use many images. Let me show you just a few
Shelly developed to deal with different situations.
When Shelly was a child, her mother responded best to her when
she was aggressive and outgoing—and so Shelly developed the
"go-getter" image. However, her father liked her best when she
was warm and soft, and so Shelly also developed the "daddy's
little girl" image. Her brothers liked her when she was tough, and
so Shelly developed a "one-of-the-guys" image. But her sister
liked it best when Shelly was sweet. And so Shelly knew how to
be "nice."

Her family didn't spend much time together except in the Social Zone. They were always doing something; there was little
time for emotions and vulnerability; and so whenever Shelly felt
anything she was branded as "moody." As a result Shelly didn't
have any well-developed images for the Personal and Intimate
Zones.

The family were practicing reformed Jews and so Shelly
needed an image that fit in; she was seen as "pious." She lived in
Florida and the climate required a "laid-back" image for adaptation to the heat. Shelly created the image of "doer" to keep her
place in the family. By the time she was in college during the
sixties it was culturally a time to be a rebel and so Shelly was
"radical." Then the feminist peer demand was for liberated
women and so Shelly complied with a "liberated" image. There
were many other images that Shelly developed, and they had all

served for a period of time, but in her present adult life most of them were out-of-date. Each of the images stayed in Shelly's memory long after she was no longer her mother's little girl, or her father's good girl, or in Florida. She had adapted, but now the situations had changed while the images remained. The problem for Shelly was that the images remained alive and forceful even when they had no productive application.

Some people naturally use the right image. When you have the right image you can walk into a party of strangers and quickly arouse interest and conversation. When you have the right image you can be in the middle of a foreign capital and feel comfortable. When you have the right image you can change a hostile negotiation into a successful contract.

Images are the acts, roles, or parts we play in life to help us adapt simultaneously to our needs and to the world around us. Remember, the self has its imperative: survival through successful adaptation. The self adapts to the different environments, situations, and people in our lives by creating an array of images. We develop different images at different times in our lives and in different situations. In the different periods of your development, different factors influenced the development of your images. You developed images in order to adapt to your mother, to your father, to your family, to your playmates, to your religion, to your schools, to your schoolmates, to the geography surrounding you, to the climate you lived in, to the economic situation you were in, to your social class, to your ethnic group, to your culture. For most interactions you are going to use an image. The question is whether or not the image is satisfying your needs.

You have images. Lots of them. Many of them you don't even know you have. By the time you have finished this chapter you are going to know what images you do have and how to create new ones, images that can help you live your life successfully in the here and now.

What is the right image? Is it being a good actor? Or pretending? *The right image is the opposite of acting. An actor recites lines, but when you have the right image you write the lines. The right image is what you do to satisfy your inner needs in the particular life zone and situation you find yourself in.*

You are using the right image when it *enhances* or *sustains* your inner reference of "you at your best." And you are using the wrong image or an out-of-date image when you find that your sense of "you at your best" is diminishing. *The right image is functional because it satisfies your needs in that life zone.*

COACH'S NOTE

The brain thinks in images. For years I was puzzled by the way people absorb complicated information. I learned the answer by studying the learning techniques employed by a world-class violinist, who has to learn one new composition after another. He told me that he dissects a new piece, bit by bit, learning one part after another. At some point his brain puts all the parts together and then he has learned it: He has in his head a complete picture of the composite parts. The brain learns through images or pictures. To work with images is to cooperate with the brain's natural information processor. If you have an image, your brain can use that image to perform many kinds of behavior, but if you know only one kind of behavior, your brain may have trouble applying it to variable circumstances. You don't learn to take a step—you learn to walk. Walking is a series of steps, but more than that, it is an image of putting steps into action that can serve many purposes.

The personality theorist George Kelly described images in technical terms this way: "Man looks at his work through transparent patterns of templates which he creates and then attempts to fit over the realities of which the world is composed." Kelly called these templates "constructs." Images not only change our view of the world but also determine what actions we take. If you are using the image of a "victim," you not only see the world as a fearful place but you act like a victim. Now that may seem difficult to understand because when you are using the "victim" image you frequently don't know it. You find yourself reacting rather than initiating action.

The right image is the image that is under the control of your self. It fills your needs and is appropriate to the zone you are in.

When you are using the right image, you aren't emotionally out of control and you know what you are actually able to do.

You don't settle for merely hoping for good results; you create good results by doing the best you can. Remember, if you are blaming someone else, looking for someone else to solve the problem, procrastinating, thinking that moving or running away will solve your problem—there is a good chance you aren't using the right image. The right image deals with the present reality. The wrong image doesn't satisfy your needs—it is a tape over which you have no control. Often you "believe" the tape because it is so loud. You forget what you can really feel like at your best. Images are like having a pair of glasses. The correct prescription expands your world while the wrong prescription distorts it.

Let me give you an example of what I mean.

Charles is a tall, slightly graying executive in his early fifties. He has a keen sense of humor, is athletic and financially successful. He owns his own company, has houses in four different cities, is known by and knows the people who are the movers and shakers in the economic and social worlds. Charles has an array of images that he uses. In the Public Zone Charles has the image of a "winner." Everything he does in the Public Zone sends out the message that Charles is a winner. When he walks down the street he smiles, is alert to what is happening around him, and makes friendly connections. In the Social Zone he has other powerful images he uses. At parties and social gatherings he has the image of "listener," "joker," and "communicator." During work hours he displays the images "successful," "in-charge," and "important."

Charles's Personal Zone and Intimate Zone images are not nearly so functional. In the Personal Zone he has tried to use the image of "communicator" but he doesn't ever talk about what he feels. To fill his needs he would have to combine "communicator" with "emotional" and express how he is feeling. Right now he is stuck with images that are not really geared to make the personal connections that would satisfy his needs. In the Intimate Zone Charles has the hardest time of all because he uses the image of "alone." No matter what happens, Charles uses his "alone" image, and it keeps him from getting what he needs. And what he needs is to be close and feel connected to someone. He can never let anyone get too close to him. He is willing to allow "liking" but rarely will he say "I love you." Charles is not unusual in having some images that work very well in some of the zones and in other zones having no images that satisfy his needs.

Charles found that he could achieve personal sync only part of the time because he was missing some important images.

Earlier I said that the *single most important* issue a person faces is whether *the self is in control of the images or the images are in control of the self.* When the self is in control, it creates images to fill your needs in all Four Life Zones. And when the images are in control, you find yourself using images that don't satisfy your needs but which are familiar and well-worn. Those images are out of date.

Compare images to a fleet of cars you own. You have a Ferrari, an old VW bug, a Chevrolet, a truck, and a station wagon. Each car is good for a specific purpose. If you try to load the entire family into the Volkswagen it isn't going to work. Or if you want to race around in the station wagon, you might find yourself in a dangerous situation. The right image is the image that fills your needs in the present based on the zone you are in.

Charles had effective images in the Public and Social Zones but was lacking functional images in the Personal and Intimate Zones. Many people have functional images in some zones but find themselves lost in other areas. People avoid those areas of life where their images aren't successful and so that life area stays weak. They are trapped between their success and their failure.

Howard was fifty-three, single, and had been the manager of his own large department store for ten years. He was a wonderful man. But his image of being "superior" was in control of his life. It made him put down everyone and everything according to standards that it had set. Howard was unaware of the superior image. He thought that what he was thinking and feeling about people was real. His self was not in control. He didn't understand why he just couldn't find the right woman. It took Howard a long time to discover that his superior image made him see the different women he met as inferior. He didn't realize that his superior image was keeping him alone and lonely.

Francine was a sensitive and warm woman. She was the mother of five children, a religious Catholic, and an active political organizer. But her image of "judge" was so strong that she seemed to take joy and excitement out of life for those she dealt with by criticizing them endlessly. She spent a lot of time wondering why her life had so little joy. Her children left home the moment they turned eighteen and her husband of twenty-five years left when he finally got up the courage to confront the "judge." Francine was hurt and disappointed with her life. She had worked hard to make her life full and satisfying, and just when she thought she would reap the benefits of her effort she found herself an exile.

Paul was a great guy, but struck people as a latter-day Napoleon. Because Paul's inadequate image was in control of his life, he resented others' successes and continually put them down. He failed to perceive why he had such trouble at work. He was a truly talented computer programmer but his bosses criticized his office manners and outlook.

Howard, Francine, and Paul are not different from the rest of us. We all recognize these unconscious self-destructive traits in others but don't see them in ourselves. These are traits that have escaped the control of the self. If the self is in control, we regularly update our images and replace the useless with new, more relevant and productive images.

How Do You Know an Image Is in Control?

You know an image is in control because you can hear it talking to you. Did you ever wonder about those little thoughts or voices you hear in your head? They are the images talking to you. Each image has a voice that vies for attention and recognition, but you make yourself unhappy when you obey them. You want to develop the voice of your self so that it becomes the guiding voice.

Exorcist Three: The Voice of the Images

Taking control over your images is not easy because your images were created to protect you. Remember, the self created the images to satisfy the imperative of "survival through successful adaptation." Old, obsolete images continue to do what they've always done and appear to resist change or your taking the reins. As you create new images your out-of-date images will rebel. They may tell you:

"It's too hard."	"You're too young."
"You're too fat."	"You're not good enough."
"You're too old."	"This is too embarrassing."

"What will others think?"

"What do you get if you do it anyway?"

"What's so good about this new behavior anyhow?"

"Someone will take advantage of you."

"It's too overwhelming."

"You just can't do this."

"You can't make me do this."

"You are lazy."

"There is not enough time."

"This is not the right time."

"It's too stressful."

"You're not strong enough to do this."

"You might fail and then what will you do?"

"It takes too much effort."

"You are too afraid."

"Other people will do it."

"You *really* are stupid."

"You will look *ridiculous.*"

"Stand up for your individuality."

"They don't understand your position."

And the number-one demon will say, "It might be O.K. for others but not for you because you and your situation are different from anyone else's situation." When you hear those comments in your head, you are really hearing just half of the story—your out-of-date image's half of the story. That's right. Every time you hear those negative comments, it is just your image trying to keep control. You learn the real story when you hear the voice of the self at the same time that you hear the voice of the image.

Out-of-Date Image Voice	*Voice of Self*
This is too scary.	This is exciting.
I'm having an anxiety attack.	I have feelings.
You have to do all this now.	Take it step by step.
Terrible things will happen.	New things will happen.
Don't do it if you don't know how.	Try new things—learning is important.
It's hopeless.	This requires effort.
If I don't know how, it will be a disaster.	If I don't know how, it will be a chance to learn.
I'm depressed.	I want to take some new action.
I'm going to commit suicide.	I am tired of not being in control.

How many times have you heard those negative and destructive voices in your head and done exactly what they told you to do? Don't despair—you just have to remember: Every time you hear an image voice in your head, you can also listen to the voice of your self. You just might need a "self hearing aid." The self sounds entirely different from the image. The self tells you what you can do, gives you encouragement and advice. The image stops you with its complaints, attacks, and criticism. The out-of-date image wants you to *talk* about what is wrong—it could be that you are fat, depressed, bothered by someone, or unhappy. But talking about it won't change it. Change takes place when you listen to the voice of the self, which will suggest a small step to try.

Listen to how tricky the voice of the out-of-date image can become. One client of mine was trying to relate to her children differently and she had an image of "being perfect." Her perfect image made her feel guilty whenever anything went wrong. I asked her if it was all right for her to be wrong. She assured me it was. And then she said, "But I just can't make a mistake." Her perfection image was splitting hairs. She could be wrong but not make mistakes. I know it may sound silly now, but she believed it. To correct this situation, I taught her to watch out for the deceitful voice of the "perfectionist."

Another client felt misunderstood. He wanted to talk about it all the time. I suggested that if he wanted to be understood, he would have to listen to what others were saying. He said to me: "You don't understand; I am misunderstood." Notice how the image wants to keep itself going. For him to change, his self had to state what it wanted. What he wanted was understanding. But to achieve this, he had to practice listening to others. He was understood as soon as his petulant "misunderstood" image lost its thrall over him. You know when an out-of-date image is talking because what it is talking about doesn't lead to action. The self takes small steady steps so that it can fill needs.

Let me give you an example. Stan was a very talented banker. When he went to work, he knew he was in the Social Zone, and his need was to work effectively and up to his potential. But then his image of the "good boy" would want one of his bosses to give him that extra "job-well-done" speech. When that didn't happen

Stan used to become negative and critical of his office. He went from wanting to be the "good boy" to being the "bad boy."

It took him a while to understand that his image was inappropriate for his present-day needs. His "good boy" image behaved as though it were certain that anyone could see what a good job he had done. In fact, he *had* done a good job; he just kept forgetting that the real reward was that it felt good to him. He already had the good feeling he was looking for. His good-boy image prevented others from seeing Stan as able to take responsibility on his own. And yet the image was so self-centered that it didn't see what it was doing.

Dr. Harold Greenwald in a June 12, 1984, *New York Times* interview said, "In a way, we're all a little like paranoids, who experience everything that goes on around them as having to do with them. To a lesser degree, everyone tends to see events as more centered on themselves than is actually the case. People experience life through a self-centered filter." Technically Dr. Greenwald calls this the "egocentric bias." In our terms, he is describing what happens when an out-of-date image is in control of the personality. If your "victim" image is in control, then you have a victim filter and bias. And if your "controller" image is in charge, then you filter and react to everything as if it needs to be controlled. You know when an image has control because its actions are repetitive.

COACH'S EXERCISE

You can start taking control over your images by interviewing them. For example, one of my clients was in love with a wonderful man. They were very happy but her images kept telling her that it was impossible for this man to love her. It told her she wasn't pretty enough, good enough, or smart enough. I taught her to interview her image. First of all she identified the image voice and then she said, "O.K., if I'm not pretty enough, smart enough, or good enough, and if I listen to you, what do I get?" The image answered, "You get to be safe." "And what does that mean?" she asked. "You won't get hurt," the image answered. "But I won't have what I want." "Yes, but you won't get hurt," replied the image. "You are lying to me, because if I don't take a chance of getting what I really want, I have hurt myself." She had taken control. The image was not bad, it was trying to protect her, but the self it was protecting was the seven-year-old girl who was never good enough, pretty enough, or smart enough for her father, not the adult woman who was smart, pretty, and good. Her image of "play it safe" was an effective image for other situations but not for the Intimate Zone in this love relationship.

Images are the players your self uses to successfully adapt to the many different situations it faces. Shelly plays many different roles in a single day. She is an executive at work, a wife and mother at home, a lover in intimate settings, and an athlete at the health club. Before she took control, she was doing what her images reacted to and not what she needed.

If you listened to why Shelly worked so much, or tried to be such a perfect mother, or why she was angry with her husband—her reasons sounded logical. But they were the twisted logic of out-of-control images and not the reasons of her self. You know they are the reasons of the images when they don't lead to satisfaction.

COACH'S NOTE

What makes distinguishing between the voice of the self and the voice of the image so difficult? The image sounds right; but it just doesn't lead anywhere. The self is always trying to satisfy your needs in the present, while the image is trying to satisfy needs you had as a child. To help yourself learn the difference, find out what need the image is trying to satisfy. Remember, it is trying to do something positive for the child-you.

Shelly's out-of-date images were out of her control because they were not focused on what she needed. She was psychologically starving to death. To help Shelly take control over her personality we started to find out what her images were in all the different life zones.

COACH'S NOTE

1. *It is O.K. to feel anything.* A feeling does not mean you have to act upon it. When you are feeling a particular emotion, identify it as an emotion. Your out-of-date image may try to make what you are feeling into the most compelling feeling. Let yourself experience your emotions as naturally as breathing. If you experience what you are feeling, then what you are feeling has a beginning, a middle, and an end. You then go on to the next experience. If you block your experience because one of your out-of-date images doesn't know how to deal with a particular emotion, then the emotion colors other experiences it has nothing to do with.

2. *Thoughts are merely thoughts.* Don't get hung up on any single thought. A thought is not to be equated with the truth; it is simply your understanding from your point of view. Make your thoughts work for you by using them as tools and not as ultimate truth. If your thoughts become your gospel, then your out-of-date images try to use them as chains to control you. If you are having trouble letting go of a thought, then you are probably stuck in an image.

3. *Behaviors are based on skill.* Don't base your judgment of yourself on a behavior you don't do well. Discover the skills you need to make your behaviors into winning behaviors.

4. *If you want the benefits of winning, you are going to have to change.* You can't win without changing.

5. *There are people who are disconnectors.* They are completely controlled by their out-of-date images and they will try to control you. Learn to avoid their image traps. Stand up to them. You know when you meet such people because your needs aren't being met. They will promise you anything in order to get you to play their game, but remember, their game is not the game of life.

6. *The reward system of the self is a state of mind.* Take control over your reward system and you can play at a championship level. The image is dependent on outside rewards.

7. *When you are feeling good there is no guarantee or certainty of permanence.* Self-esteem comes when you are willing to live with good feeling in the moment, knowing you can always find it again.

8. *The more you take control, the more intensity you will feel.* Intensity gives you access to pleasure. Intensity is what you want and what your out-of-date images fear. Out-of-date images tell you that intensity is bad and to move away from it. Self uses intensity to master life.

9. *The better you start feeling, the more you will fear losing that good feeling.* Just remember, it is your image that is really afraid. Your self likes feeling better.

10. *You have to challenge your images.* Are they as effective today as they were yesterday? Or are they out-of-date?

11. *Images are like tapes and they are useful only to the extent of what has been recorded onto them.* You are not your images. You are the person who created them. You can edit them, throw them out, and decide how you will use them.

12. *Images are supposed to be useful, so practice them, train them, make them work for you.* This is what world-class athletes do and you can do the same.

CHAPTER
·17·

The Image Checklist

I am going to list some common images for you to choose from in each of the four zones. Put a check following those images you are using in each zone. You may even be using the same image in each of the Four Life Zones. AN IMPORTANT POINT TO REMEMBER: IMAGES ARE NOT GOOD OR BAD, POSITIVE OR NEGATIVE. THEY ARE EITHER USEFUL TO YOU NOW OR NOT USEFUL. The images listed are just a few of those frequently used.

	Public	*Social*	*Personal*	*Intimate*
Crusader				
Victim				
Negative				
Argumentative				
Critical				
Child				
Parent				
Know-it-all				
Fearful				
Lost				
Loser				
Important				
Nice Guy/Gal				
Joker				
Space Cadet				

	Public	Social	Personal	Intimate
Positive				
Powerhouse				
Athlete				
Communicator				
Listener				
Risker				
Dependable				
Lover				
Wimp				
Macho				
Achiever				
Enjoyer				
Hard Worker				
Winner				
Show-Off				
Stupid				
Not Good Enough				
Perfectionist				
Bully				
Inferior				
Seductive				
Lecturer				
Vulnerable				
Sensitive				
Giver				
Thoughtful				
Receiver				

Now go back over the list and circle an image you would like to change in each of the four zones. Write it here.

Images I Want to Change

Public Zone Image _____

Social Zone Image _____

Personal Zone Image _____

Intimate Zone Image _____

Shelly and I went over scores of different images. For each image she was using in the different life zones we identified how effective the image was. We asked: "Does this image fill your need in this zone?"

You can do the same for yourself by answering the following questions for each image that you checked.

1. When did I create this image?
2. What were my inner needs when I created it?
3. What were the outer demands on me when I created it?
4. How strong was my self when I created it?
5. What were my other options at that time?

When you answer these questions you are going to discover that each image you created was probably the best possible adaptation you could have made at that moment. The image may not work now, however, because it doesn't satisfy the needs of your adult self in the present moment.

COACH'S NOTE

You are going to be using different images all your life. What will change is how much control you have over those images and how effectively those images satisfy your needs.

Here is the same list of images with an analysis of how the image is appropriate for the adult self.

Coach's Image Analysis

Crusader: This image is very good for working at causes, especially in the Public Zone. It becomes less effective in the Social Zone because people get tired of hearing about the crusade. And it is absolutely lethal in the Personal and Intimate Zones. People who use the image of crusader for personal needs in a relationship will find resentment from the others in their lives.

Victim: The victim image is not effective in any one of the Four Life Zones. The victim image is usually a cover-up for the power image. The victim always selects someone to take the role of victimizer and thus become "the victim's victim." What most people don't realize is that at one time in their lives they were in a victim's position—as children. The feeling is real; it is the time that is wrong.

Negative: This image works in specific situations in the Public Zone, for example, pointing out the dangers of radioactive waste and toxic chemicals. But even then the negative image must be kept in check because it rarely motivates action on the part of others. In the Social Zone the negative image can be useful when someone or something is overly positive. But generally the negative image is not effective. The negative image in the Personal and Intimate Zones is counterproductive. A version of the negative image is the complainer.

Argumentative: This is a great image for the Social Zone, especially for trial lawyers and high-school debaters. However, it can easily get out of hand because it is always looking for things to argue about. It is clearly not an image for the Personal and Intimate Zones. If you are going to use this image, you had better combine it with the funny image and the caring image to make it effective.

Critical: This is a terrific image for the Public Zone in limited situations such as political analysis, film criticism, and restaurant reviews. In the Social Zone it is an excellent image for lawyers, editors, scientists, and chefs. It is absolutely inappropriate for the Personal and Intimate Zones. If you use the critical image in a relationship, you are going to find yourself in an unhappy and hostile situation. A relationship is for support and change, not criticism and browbeating.

Child: This is an image everyone seems to use in at least one of the four zones—and it doesn't work. It is a carryover from the past. The image suggests that if you are a child, someone will take care of you. That is a lie. No matter how much of a child you are or how much someone takes care of you, the image only builds resentment.

Parent: This is the counterpart to the child image. The parent image works well if you are raising a family, serving as a crossing guard at a grade school, or teaching kindergarten; but otherwise it may come across as condescending or controlling and, in a word, inappropriate.

Know-it-all: This image doesn't work and it is strange how many people use it. Doctors use it more than others, but lawyers and college professors also seem to relish it. It is a no-no in the Personal and Intimate Zones. It doesn't work unless someone is busy being your student. If you hear yourself knowing it all, back off and start listening to what others have to say.

Fearful: This image works in the Public Zone in those situations that are actually dangerous. It may occasionally be an ineffective image in the Social Zone, and there are times when sharing the fearful image in the Personal and Intimate Zones is especially good for breaking down barriers. But in general the fearful image promises that if you run away you will feel better than if you took a chance. That is hardly ever true.

Lost: This image conveys the idea that a person just doesn't know what is going on. It is amazing just how good the lost image is at finding other people to lead the way and take the chances. Remember, to be "lost" effectively, you have to know where you are going. You can use the lost image effectively during a critical negotiation in the Social Zone by getting the other person to explain again and again what is going on. Before you know it, he has become tired of you and gives in as soon as you switch to argumentative. Like the Trojan horse, you have snuck behind his image. This image is a total disaster in the Personal and Intimate Zones.

Loser: This is a very common image whenever someone believes he is a loser and nothing he does will work. But if it works for a moment it will fail in the long run. This image promises that if a person only felt more, understood more, or was more sensitive, he or she would be more effective. It's a lie.

Important: This is an excellent image in all four zones. In the Public Zone this image will help you find out vital facts and get through red tape. In the Social Zone it is effective if it is combined with the hard worker image and communicator image. In the Personal Zone it is excellent for communicating your need for respect and equality. And in the Intimate Zone it lets you know you are good enough to be loved and good enough to love.

Nice Guy/Gal: This image works well in all four zones if it is limited in its use. There must be some depth and assertiveness behind the nice guy/gal image; otherwise it becomes superficial and boring.

Joker: This image works well in all four zones as long as it is accompanied by more substantial images. Otherwise, it becomes defensive and counterproductive.

Space Cadet: This image works in the Social Zone for geniuses. The space cadet gets other people to work hard to understand him or her. The only problem is that people get tired of doing that unless they are also space cadets. It is completely inappropriate in the Public, Personal, and Intimate Zones.

Positive: This image works well in all four zones. It is vital to keeping you aware of your ability to get what you need, and it helps to prevent you from being sidetracked by other people's negative images.

Powerhouse: This image works well in the Social Zone. It is especially suited for work and sports. It must be balanced with a sensitive image; otherwise it can become dominating and overbearing.

Athlete: This image works well in all Four Life Zones. It lets you bring energy and excitement to whatever you are doing. The only real difficulty with the athlete image is knowing when to stop using it.

Communicator: This is a great image in all Four Life Zones because the communicator is not trying to be right but simply learning how to connect. The communicator doesn't take disagreements personally but simply as forms of miscommunication. To work really well, the communicator needs to be coupled with the listener image.

Listener: Like the communicator, this image works in all Four Life Zones. It needs to be coupled with the communicator to be really effective.

Risker: This image is powerful and effective in all Four Life Zones. In each zone it allows for different kinds of risks. It must, however, be coupled with the dependable image; otherwise the risks become meaningless and dangerous.

Dependable: This image is at its best in the Social Zone. If you are dependable, you are able to fill many of your Social Zone needs. In the other zones it adds to the quality of the other dominant images of those zones. This is a great image for a Personal Zone friendship.

Lover: This image works moderately well in the Public and Social Zones, but it is outstanding in the Personal and Intimate Zones. You are a lover when you take the time and exert the effort to gain insight and show your care to someone you love. The more you use this image in the Personal and Intimate Zones, the more your needs and the needs of those you love can be filled.

Wimp: This image doesn't work, although many people use it. It is the image that won't let you speak up, take a chance, or risk any new behavior.

Macho: This is an overworked and abused image in the Social Zone. It is used most often in sports, but it finds its way into every aspect of all four zones. This image is out-of-date culturally. Macho is a parody of masculinity.

Achiever: This is a great image in the Social Zone. It is inappropriate in most cases in the other three zones. It can become a liability if it is not coupled with the enjoyer image.

Enjoyer: This image is excellent for all four zones if it is coupled with a different and appropriate image in each of those zones. For example, in the Social Zone, enjoyer-achiever is an effective image; in the Personal Zone, enjoyer-communicator is a need-satisfying image; and the enjoyer-lover is a fantastic Intimate Zone image.

Hard Worker: This image is excellent for the Social and Personal Zones but not for the Public and Intimate Zones. The hard worker can get carried away with hard work. It needs to be coupled with an image like enjoyer.

Winner: This image is one of the best for the Social Zone. If it is coupled with nice guy/gal and joker, it is a powerful way to satisfy Social Zone needs.

Show-off: This is a fun image for specific situations like parties in the Social Zone. Other than that, it is very limited and totally inappropriate for the other zones.

Stupid: This is an image everyone seems to use at times except those who have the cover-up image of the know-it-all. The stupid image doesn't work in any zone and is a protective mechanism against taking responsibility for one's own thoughts. Remember, if you find yourself using this image, that you have a great deal of knowledge in some fields. It isn't necessary to be knowledgeable about everything, but you can learn more if you want to.

Not Good Enough: This image is very prevalent and is not effective in any of the life zones. If you find yourself thinking you are not good enough, ask "Not good enough for whom?" You will find that you are still relating to someone in your past.

Perfectionist: This image is excellent for brain surgeons and copy editors. It is deadly in the hands of anyone else. Everyone seems to use this image at times but it doesn't satisfy needs in any zone. Sit back and think about how inflated this image is. Perfection is a game of infinity. We are finite, and perfection is outside our realm. The lie of the perfectionist image is: "If everything were perfect and the way I wanted it to be, then I'd be happy." Remember, it is a seductive image but still a lie.

Bully: This image works well in limited sports events and some work situations, both of which are in the Social Zone. Otherwise this image doesn't work and often only gets more aggressive when it doesn't get its way.

Inferior: A version of not good enough and stupid, the inferior image doesn't work and it feels bad about it. If you think you are inferior, then you are trapped by an image that doesn't work well. Take a good look at it and then make the decision to retire it.

Seductive: This image is a wonderful image for all four zones. But it can, like any image, get out of hand. When it is combined with the image of dependable or lover, it is not only effective, it is a joy.

Lecturer: This is a very typical male image. Ask him a question and before you know it you are getting a lecture on the meaning of the universe. This image doesn't work well except in the Social Zone and in a classroom. It doesn't work at all in the Personal and Intimate Zones.

Vulnerable: This is a terrific image in the Personal and Intimate Zones. It lets people know they have a place in your life. If you seem impenetrable, you may find yourself missing out on the rewards of the Personal and Intimate Zones.

Sensitive: When this image is used in the Public Zone, it is a disaster. But in the Social Zone, when combined with achiever, it is a powerhouse. Sensitive is a required image for the Personal and Intimate Zones.

Giver: This image works well in all Four Life Zones. If you are a giver, you are going to find people welcoming you into their lives. The opposite of the giver is the taker—the more you take the less you get. Remember, to get anything from other people you must let them give it to you.

Thoughtful: This is a great image for all Four Life Zones. If you don't take the time to think about other people's positions and feelings and needs, you are going to miss the essence of being with them—them. If you are thoughtful, you get the reward of knowing people as they are.

Receiver: This image works well in all Four Life Zones. It means you are willing to receive what other people have to give you. Nothing feels better in the Public Zone than to smile at someone and have the smile reciprocated. The same goes for the other life zones.

These images we have reviewed are only a small part of your image army. As you grow and mature you will find that you have the skill and opportunity to create just the right image at just the right time. You will no longer be forced to use an out-of-date image that doesn't fill your needs or those of the people you are interacting with.

In Chapter Eighteen we will find out how to create new images using needs and the Four Life Zones.

COACH'S NOTE

Remember, your obsolete images often seem to have a life, a personality, and a will of their own.

1. Images don't want you to get what *you* want. They want you to long for it but not to have it. They want what *they* want.
2. Images get you to do things because of how they look and not how they feel.
3. Images want you to quit and run away in difficult situations. The self wants to stay and learn. Out-of-date images fear failure while the self knows that failure is not to be feared.
4. Images are willing to keep you from getting what you want as long as they can remain in control.
5. Images will never identify themselves, admit their shortcomings, or seek to change.
6. Images will try to control the intensity of others through judgment and nonparticipation. You don't have to judge oth-

ers unless they are in a beauty contest. Let others judge themselves through their actions.

7. Success is dependent on knowing what you need even if you don't know how to satisfy that need. You must step into the unfamiliar with a positive outlook. Images lead you to believe that success always occurs in the familiar and the known.

8. Take control over your images by identifying them when they try to control you. See what their trigger points are and what their limitations are. Don't let your images bully you.

9. You are not guilty for what you have not learned. Your out-of-date images try to make you feel guilty for what you have done or what you are trying to change. This is a control ploy.

10. Understanding is not the same as doing something. Your out-of-date images will try to get you to settle for understanding when it is action that makes you feel good. They will tell you that you could do it if you tried—but that you don't have to try.

11. If your self-esteem is low it means your out-of-date images are in control. Don't get trapped into trying to solve problems when you simply need to remove the images from power.

12. Out-of-date images try to make reality simple. Reality is complex and deep. Your self is willing to live without knowing the parameters of reality. Your out-of-date images live in a black-and-white world.

13. Your out-of-date images get angry at someone who makes a mistake or doesn't do something the way you would do it. The image is actually using the other person to control you. The self responds to others as they are, and when someone else makes a mistake it either helps them correct it or gets out of the way. To react to others with anger only diverts them from their course and moves them into a defensive position.

14. Despair is the result of not learning. If you take the best action you can take at the moment and you find out tomorrow that it wasn't effective and you feel guilty about it—you are in the cycle of despair. You haven't learned. Learning should take place no matter what action you take; it doesn't always have to be correct.

15. Guilt is a poor substitute for learning. You feel guilty about what you did yesterday even though you couldn't have known then what you know today. Now, because of the action you took then, you have gained knowledge. Your job is to live and learn.

·18·

How to Create
the Right Image

Once people understand the nature of their images, they often want to drop the old ones and adopt new ones. They want to get rid of the depressed image, the loser image, and the victim image. But that is only half the story. To be effective in life you need a wardrobe of images that are appropriate for the Four Life Zones and your needs. A new image can galvanize your inner resources and take you into those areas where your new adult-need satisfaction lies.

But how do you do it? There is a recipe to follow:

Step 1: Identify your need or your goal.
Step 2: Identify what zone you are in.
Step 3: Review your old images. Ask if they work for your new need or goal.
Step 4: Blend two or more new images to create an image to fill your need or accomplish your goal.
Step 5: Now use "you at your best" as a guidepost for the new image.

If the image enhances your feeling of "you at your best," then it is a functional and effective image. If it diminishes that feeling, then it is nonfunctional and ineffective. Remember, we aren't looking for an image that works just on the outside. We are trying to create images that work effectively in the world and keep us centered on our inner reference of our best.

When Shelly stood up to the executive who was trying to undermine her projects, she was able to do that because she had developed a new work image. Let me show you how we did this. Shelly had been talking about wanting to be different at work. And so we went through the image-creating recipe.

Step 1: What do you need?

Shelly answered this question by saying she needed to be more successful, to break through the "old boys' club barrier" and get a promotion.

Step 2: What zone are you in?

Shelly said this need was in the Social Zone at work. Here is where she and I did most of our work. Shelly was suffering from zone confusion. She kept taking the competition, the opposition, and the demands at work personally. She was using Personal Zone rules and regulations in the Social Zone. Those people who wanted to keep her from moving ahead were keeping her emotionally unbalanced by their putdowns.

Step 3: Review your old images.

Shelly reviewed her old images and found they were those of "victim," "helpless," "worker," "good, but not great." None of these images would work for Shelly's need. She needed a new image.

Step 4: Blend two or more images to create a new and effective image.

Shelly and I reviewed all the different images and we found that "sensitive-winner" worked for her. As a sensitive-winner she had access to all her feminine qualities and yet the competitive will and strength of action that a winner has. She wrote the image out on a card. She thought about it. And she began to guide her work actions by using the sensitive-winner image. Before long Shelly was performing like a winner. Remember, a new image focuses your attention in a particular situation in a new way. In this case, the focus was on attaining her goal and not on the personal interactions.

Step 5: Use "you at your best" as a guide to test the new image.

Shelly tested this new image by using her enhance-sustain-diminish compass. She found that when she used the sensitive-winner at work she was enhancing herself. And whenever she started to feel bad, it was because an out-of-date image had taken over at work.

Clients and I go through this time and again. They consciously create new images that satisfy their needs. But to meet those needs they have to know what life zone they are in and the image they create must be guided from within.

Many people want to be real, to be their real selves in the real world. But when they try to be this "real" self, they often substitute their version of reality for the world. If they feel angry on the tennis court, then that is real, and if they don't feel like working, then that is real, and if they don't want to be sensitive, then that is real. Reality, however, is about successful survival and growth. It is about what is happening not only within you but between you and others.

When most people talk about being real they are trying to stop the world and make it the way they want it to be. They are playing games. They will confound, procrastinate, subvert, confuse the real goals in order to feel that they are in control. These people are not life-athletes; they are game players. And the games they are playing are image games. As a coach I warn clients: Be careful what you try to win—you just might. Your success should be guided by your inner sense of "you at your best." Your success should feel good each step of the way.

Once you create a successful image, don't overdo it. Remember, you have needs in all four zones. If you deprive yourself in any of the four zones, what began as success becomes a stumbling block. As you get good at creating successful new images, you no longer worry about how long your success will last. You don't create a success and then hang on for dear life. You didn't become successful by hanging on; you got there by creating a new and effective image. Let's go on and create some new images for you in each of the four zones.

Creating New Public Zone Images

Coach's Questions

1. What was your score in the Public Zone: Self-confident, Confident, or Shy? (Circle one)

2. What were the three main needs you *didn't* get satisfied in the Public Zone?

a. _____

b. _____

c. _____

Image Recipe

Step One: Identify your need or your goal. _____
_____
_____
_____

Step Two: Identify what zone you are in. _____

Step Three: Review your old images. Do they work for this new need or goal? _____
_____

Step Four: Blend two or more images to create an image that would be effective.

Image one _____
Image two _____
Image three _____
New image _____

Step Five: Now use "you at your best" as the benchmark or guidepost for the new image.

Once you have gone through these five steps, you need to spend time thinking about, visualizing, and imagining the feelings, sensations, and changes that would result from creating this new image and getting new results. Remember, you are used to not getting what you want. With your new image you will get what you want and you are going to have to be prepared for the results you want.

Creating New Social Zone Images

Coach's Questions

1. Was your score Self-esteem, Worried but Willing, or Down but Not Out? (Circle one)

2. What were the three main needs you *didn't* get satisfied in this zone?
   a. _____
   b. _____
   c. _____

Image Recipe

Step One: Identify your need or your goal. _____
_____
_____
_____

Step Two: Identify what zone you are in. _____

Step Three: Review your old images. Do they work for this new need or goal? _____
_____

Step Four: Blend two or more images to create an image that would be effective.

Image one _____
Image two _____
Image three _____
New image _____

Step Five: Now use "you at your best" as the benchmark or guidepost for the new image.

Once you have gone through these five steps, you need to spend time thinking about, visualizing, and imagining the feelings, sensations, and changes that would result from creating this new image and getting new results. Remember, you are used to not getting what you want. With your new image you will get what you want and you are going to have to be prepared for the results you want.

Creating New Personal Zone Images

Coach's Questions

1. Was your score Self-worth, Almost There, Needs a Self-worth Charge? (Circle one)

2. What were the three main needs you *didn't* get satisfied in this zone?
   a. _____
   b. _____
   c. _____

Image Recipe

Step One: Identify your need or goal. _____
_____
_____
_____

Step Two: Identify what zone you are in. _____

Step Three: Review your old images. Do they work for this new need or goal? _____
_____

Step Four: Blend two or more images to create an image that would be effective.

Image one _____

Image two _____

Image three _____

New image _____

Step Five: Now use "you at your best" as the benchmark or guidepost for the new image.

Once you have gone through these five steps, you need to spend time thinking about and visualizing the feelings and changes that would result from creating this new image and getting new results. Remember, you are used to not getting what you want. With your new image you will get what you want and you are going to have to be prepared for the results you want.

Creating New Intimate Zone Images

Coach's Questions

1. Was your result Self-love, Lovable, or Heartbroken? (Circle one)

2. What were the three main needs you *didn't* get satisfied in this zone?

a. _____

b. _____

c. _____

Image Recipe

Step One: Identify your need or your goal. _____

_____

_____

_____

Step Two: Identify what zone you are in. _____

Step Three: Review your old images. Do they work for this new need or goal? _____
_____

Step Four: Blend two or more images to create an image that would be effective.

        Image one _____
        Image two _____
        Image three _____
        New image _____

Step Five: Now use "you at your best" as the benchmark or guidepost for the new image.

Once you have gone through these five steps, you need to spend time thinking about and visualizing the feelings and changes that would result from creating this new image and getting new results. Remember, you are used to not getting what you want. With your new image you will get what you want and you are going to have to be prepared for the results you want.

You will naturally put your new image into action and receive the concomitant benefits. Creating a new image makes it possible to climb mountains that seemed insurmountable before. You can cross new frontiers in your life. What has happened in the past and what is happening now does not have to be what will happen in the future—because you have taken new action. Your new action started when you identified your real problem for the first time—an old image wasn't working well. And you changed it.

In the next chapter we will learn to send the right signals. Once you can send and receive the right signals, you have put it all together. You'll be in sync.

COACH'S NOTE
_____

   1. The difference between an out-of-date and a functional image is that an out-of-date image believes itself immortal and has a life of its own, while a functional image is there to do a job—to satisfy needs of the self.

2. Each image (functional or out-of-date) has a unique view of reality. Learn to use the perspective of the image without using it as a reality. Your final check with reality must be yourself.

3. In business situations figure out what images other people are using. Then figure whether or not the other person has control over his or her images. This insight will give you an inestimable advantage.

4. Your out-of-date images will lie to you by making promises they can't keep. Don't let yourself be seduced by them. You'll know this is happening when you make mistakes and overreact.

5. Talking too much or too little offers a hint that you are being controlled by an image. The image isn't paying attention to what is happening outside of you. Instead, it is just playing its tape.

6. Images deal with the picture of things, not the reality. The image plays a stage drama; the self plays the real game of life.

7. Out-of-date images make repetitive errors.

8. Your images will determine how people will relate to you.

9. Don't get caught in your own image game. The image is one of your players, not you yourself.

10. Get out of the way of other people's out-of-date images, overreactions, and mistakes. You don't have to respond to their errors.

Section Six

THE RIGHT SIGNALS

CHAPTER

·19·

The Signals You Send

How do you stay in the right place once you have found it? Do you invite someone over into your Intimate Zone? Do you ask "Are we in the Social or the Personal Zone?" Or is it "Excuse me. I think you are stepping into my Personal Zone"? There is something that you can do to stay in the right place. Some people already know how to do it. And the rest of us can learn quickly.

Jeannie ran a classroom like no other teacher in the school. Her students were energetic, motivated, and eager to try. It was just the right place.

Howard had been sales manager for only twenty months and in that time sales had increased by 35 percent. His salespeople were willing to work above and beyond the call of duty. He had that something special.

Jennifer had the touch. Everything she touched at the advertising agency turned to pure gold. Her co-workers liked and respected her and they knew she was going to succeed. She was considered special.

Brian was the best insurance agent his company had seen in the last fifteen years. He sold more policies than anyone else in the country and he didn't look as if he'd tried. Everyone thought he was one of those lucky few.

Jeannie, Howard, Jennifer, and Brian are *not* special. They *don't* have more talent. They are *not* lucky. And what they have you can learn. *What they know is how to read and send the right signals.*

Not long ago Jeannie thought that the next time a child got out of line, asked a stupid question, or had a runny nose she would start screaming. Jeannie's classes used to be like those of every other teacher who has problems. The children didn't pay attention. Jeannie used to get frustrated with the children, and then she would get down on herself. When she first came to see me, she wanted to know what was wrong with her. She wanted to know how to uncover the secrets of her personality so that she could put up with the "little monsters." What she told me made me realize that Jeannie's problems were not inside her but in the signals she was sending and receiving. Let's go over what she and I found out.

School takes place in the Social Zone. In school, children are expected to perform the activity of learning. But school isn't just about learning. It is the place where children bring all their problems from home, it is where children are learning how to socialize with other children and unfamiliar adults, and school is full of failure. It wasn't that the children in Jeannie's class weren't paying attention to school and learning, but they had many different things on their minds. They sent Jeannie signals not only from the Social Zone but from the Personal Zone—"I am sad," "Nobody likes me"—and from the Intimate Zone—"I love you."

Jeannie's signals ranged from the cheerleader in the Public Zone to the mother in the Personal Zone. The kids were sending and receiving what family therapists call mixed messages. Jeannie and I worked on learning to identify the different signals the children were sending. Once we could do this, Jeannie learned to respond appropriately to the children's signals. She was able to respond (she took the time) to the personal signals the kids sent and to their social signals. She was like an air-traffic controller, guiding each of the little planes onto the runways and off again.

Many teachers don't know how to reach their children and so the children start to get unruly. Children can't pay attention when *their* signals are not being responded to. When a teacher can identify a child's signals and respond, the teacher has that child's attention. For Jeannie this meant teaching her children that she would set aside time for them and their personal needs.

Once the children knew there would be time for sorting out what was going on in their heads, it was much easier for them to pay attention to school. The teacher sometimes is the only person in a child's life who is able to receive and respond to his or her signals.

A few years ago Howard was stuck waiting on tables. He was a successful waiter and then a successful salesman, but when he became sales manager he was lost. Instead of asking people what they wanted, he began trying to tell them what to do. His signals were unclear and often demotivating. When you think about it, most managers don't know the first thing about human signals. Howard and I analyzed the situation at his office, and we discovered that his success as a waiter and a salesman came from listening to what someone wanted and then helping him get it. We applied the same logic to his sales-manager job. He started sending out the signal that he wanted to know what his salespeople wanted and that he would help them get it. Sometimes what the salespeople wanted was a sympathetic "I know how tough it is," and at other times they wanted "Get out there and do it! I know you can." Howard became a great sales manager because he learned to send and receive the right signals.

Jennifer was always creative but she could never keep a job. Every time she went to work she sent off signals that she was creative and couldn't be bothered with anybody else. It turned out that nobody else could be bothered with her either. She and I analyzed just how she lost jobs and why. We discovered that she often intimidated others with her signals. She didn't realize what it was like to be in the room with someone as creative and energetic as she was. She learned to change the signals she sent so that others felt included and needed. Jennifer enhanced her creativity by getting others to be creative. It was then that her creative powers took off. People were sharing good ideas with her and improving on good ideas because Jennifer was sending signals that were warm and friendly, exciting and welcoming.

Brian was a throwback to another era. He loved to give personal service. His problem was that he gave too much of it. He sent the signal to his clients that he was always there for them. And before long, Brian was spending more time going out for dinner and having a quick lunch than he was selling insurance.

We took his strong and caring signal and added a professional touch to it. People bought insurance from him and let him live his own life.

All these people have learned how to send and receive the right signals.

Mary, a client of mine, told me the following story. She and her husband were in their bedroom talking about what had happened that day. Mary started to feel very loving and warm toward her husband, she knew she had a need to express that love, and she found a "lover" image to fill those needs. She sent the signals of "intimacy" through the tone of her voice, her touch, and what she talked about. She could have continued talking about her day, but then she would have been sending social signals. Mary was in sync with her needs and the right signals.

Signals are the basic human connectors, like the couplings on a freight train. If the freight cars are not connected, it doesn't matter that the engine is ready or that the cars are loaded with the precious cargo—*nothing happens until the connection occurs.* It is as common and yet as complex as making a phone call—communication cannot take place until the connection is made—but you have to know how to dial the number and receive the call if you want to connect. Most important, you have to know how to dial many different numbers with different area codes.

The right signals harmonize zone, need, and image and assist in creating total synchrony. Just imagine being on a lake. It is a crystal-clear fall morning, the sun is coming up, your favorite hunting dog is by your side, you are dressed in camouflage fatigues, you have your best shotgun loaded, and then you see the ducks come swooping in over the horizon. You are at the right place, at the right time, with the right image. You seem to be in perfect sync—and then you start playing loud rock-and-roll music over outdoor speakers. The ducks fly off. Wrong signals. Pffftt!

Come on. It has happened in one way or another to all of us. And to you, too. How many times have you found yourself in just the right place with the right opportunity—only to see it evaporate?

You are there at that intimate moment, you feel sexually excited and aroused, and the next moment it is as if you had never met the other person. You can't figure out what happened. That happened to Veronica. She was in bed with her husband, getting ready to make love, and the next moment he rolled over and went to sleep. She didn't find out why until the next morning.

You finally get the job interview with the company where you have wanted to work for years, your résumé is right, and you look fantastic. But right from the start the interview is off, not quite right. You can't figure out why what you said had no impact. That also happened to a client of mine. She didn't learn why she lost the job until she met an old friend in a bar six months later.

You are talking with your child. He has been having trouble at school and is reacting to your questions with anger and denial. You have finally found that moment when the two of you are riding in the car alone and you feel close. You start to talk and then the moment never really happens. This occurred with a client of mine. He and his son were talking about what it means to be macho and finally to be able to love each other as father and son, and then his son got up and walked away.

Were those times illusions? Was it just by chance that they missed out—and you missed out in similar circumstances? What's happening here? What happened in each of the cases was that the wrong signals were sent. The woman wanting to make love with her husband sent a negative cautionary signal that he had better be sensitive when what she had really intended to convey was that she was excited. A missed signal. The woman looking for the job found out she hadn't sent a signal of respect. And the man sent his son the signal "this is information" rather than staying with more loving signals, and so his son could not have cared less. Finding and staying in the right place are vital if you are to send and receive the right signals.

The Wrong Signals

There are some very common wrong signals that will cause you to disconnect from someone without your ever realizing what happened.

Withdrawal: If you are connected with someone—no matter how difficult the situation—and you want to succeed, you have to keep from withdrawing. When you withdraw you are sending a negative signal. The other person thinks either that he or she

has done something wrong or that there is something wrong
with you. What is usually wrong is something that requires the
two of you to change.

Defensiveness: This is a signal that never works. By the time
you are defensive you are either letting someone get away with
attacking you or putting yourself in a one-down position. Defensiveness as a signal says there is something wrong. You have to
believe in what you are doing—even though you are willing to
change.

Accusation: This is a common negative signal. It doesn't work.
When you accuse someone of anything, the only natural response
is to send back a defensive or attacking signal. Watch your accusations—it is most likely a sign you are in the wrong zone.

Self-chauvinist: This signal says "me, me, me, me." You talk
about yourself, direct and redirect all that is happening toward
yourself. A self-chauvinist signal is nothing less than a reason for
someone else to disconnect, even if he or she may have to sit
through the rest of the dinner with you.

Double messages: This is the basis for making someone
crazy. Yes, I'll do the job but not the way you want me to. Yes, I
love you but don't come close. Yes, I am your friend but I don't
have time for you. Yes, we are a family, but we don't show affection. Yes, I love you but I'm just not sexual. Yes, you deserve a
promotion but you're not ready for it. Yes, you did a good job
but there was a mistake.

Character assassination: If you want to send a strong negative and disconnecting signal—then attack another person's character. Think you understand them, why they act, why they don't,
and then tell them so. When you embark upon character assassination, the cadaver lying there is bound to be yours.

Eye disconnect: If you can't and don't look at someone, you
are sending a signal that says "I can't stand looking at you,"
"There isn't much to look at," or "I am afraid to look."

Physical disconnect: If you don't know how to use your
body to show physical affection, you are physically disconnecting. Your body is either talking or not talking.

Dependency: This signal is a major disconnector and most
people are unaware they are sending it. The dependency signal is
one that makes the other person responsible for your happiness
or success. When you send a dependency signal you are saying

that you can't sustain yourself and that the other person must take care of you rather than participate with you.

Selfish sexual signals: This signal says "I want sex for me, right now" or the reverse, "I don't want sex right now." In either case there is no connection and contact. Sexual signals require tact and care for your own vulnerability and the vulnerability of the other person.

Signals in Action

It took one failure after another before Nathan learned how to send the right signals. Nathan was a television-commercial director, and a producer who was a source of many jobs for Nathan was very difficult to connect with. If Nathan called, the man would put him off by telling him to call back. When he did, the man would offer to meet with him next week. Nathan used to get furious. He wanted to tell the man off with the classic "Who do you think you are?" For years that is just what Nathan had done with other people in his life. He had done it with his first wife, his children, his second wife, and everyone he had worked with. It is interesting that even though he knew he was in the right place, he knew what he needed, and he possessed functional images, he was nonetheless unaware of the signals he was sending. He just couldn't understand why others reacted so negatively. *What he didn't know was that to get in sync required learning how to connect with people by sending and receiving the right signals.*

Nathan used to think that if he only said what he meant, everyone would understand him. And he used to be certain that he understood what other people were saying. He finally learned to stop speaking his private language and to send and receive signals other people could use to connect with him. He discovered that by listening to the troublesome producer carefully, by not taking things personally, and by responding exactly to what the man said, he got appointments. In fact, he was getting appointments while other people were spending their time complaining.

Nathan learned how to read signals. The producer always sent three signals before he connected. The first two were "put off" signals and the third was a confirmed meeting. We often assume that just because people speak the same language, they are communicating with us. That is a lethal and losing assumption. Before you can communicate, you have to connect, and the way to connect is to assess carefully the signals you're receiving and sending.

Signal Disruptors: The Deadly Little *Mises*

Nathan learned to stay in sync by not taking all the little *mis*es personally. People often don't realize when they have been disconnected by a little *mis*. They *mis*perceive a communication. They *mis*communicate. They *mis*understand a communication. They *mis*understand their own perception. They *mis*perceive a *mis*communication. They *mis*understand a *mis*understanding. They *mis*perceive a *mis*perception. They *mis*communicate a *mis*communication. The little *mis*es are deadly. When you have a *mis* you disconnect. When you send and receive the right signals you connect. Signals are like any foreign language. Communication is awkward until you begin to think in that language. Once you learn about signals, they will become second nature. There is *not one* couple I work with who really know *consistently* how to send and receive the right signals. The women tend to think men are speaking some Neanderthal language, and the men tend to think the women are speaking emotional gibberish. At the most basic level men want to fix it, rebuild it, do something, while the women want to feel it, incubate it, share it. The signals get lost in the blame and accusation. Change is possible. You don't have to be trapped by anybody else's signals or your own.

COACH'S NOTE: HOW TO READ OTHER PEOPLE'S SIGNALS

Here are some coaching tips on reading other people's signals. Whenever someone else is sending you a signal, take the time to read it before responding to the words. If you don't, you may find yourself responding in unproductive ways. For example, you may be in a negotiation for an important deal and the other people are sending you the message "We are friends and this is personal" when in fact, you aren't friends and it isn't personal. If you can't pick up the signal, you will find yourself responding *as if* you were in a contest the other person had initiated. The same for sympathy, power, position, or sex. Make sure you know what signal is being sent. Is the signal

connect/disconnect?
action/nonaction?
present/future?
present/past?
friendly/unfriendly?
fearful/confident?

If you start noticing the quality of the signals other people are sending, you can analyze them in relation to the words they are using. Match the sound of the voice with the feelings. Match their body language with your natural response. The more carefully you study the signals someone is sending, the more accurately you can respond.

The 100 Percent Theory

To help Shelly stay in the right place I taught her the 100 percent theory. In the 100 percent theory you assume that other people are perfect in what they are doing, and it is 100 percent up to you to find out what signals will make the connection. Of course, no one is ever sending out entirely accurate signals, but the 100 percent theory says you don't have control over others but you do have control over yourself. If you take 100 percent control over what you are doing, then your chances of staying in the right place go up dramatically. If you don't take 100 percent control, then your chances of connecting go down drastically.

If, for example, 25 percent of the time you are sending the right signal and others are misreading it, 25 percent of the time you are sending the wrong signal and they are reading it correctly, or 25 percent of the time you are sending the wrong signal and they are misreading it, then there remains only 25 percent chance that you will be sending the right signal and someone else will be reading it correctly. After a while you don't know who is doing what.

COACH'S NOTE

Don't take miscommunication, misperception, misunderstanding, or disconnection personally. Take very personally communication, perception, understanding, and connecting.

If you want to stay in sync, stop worrying about who is right or wrong—your job is to stay connected and in the right zone. If you are more concerned with being right than staying in sync, you are going to find yourself smack in the wrong place at the wrong time. In the next chapter we'll find out about sending the right signals.

COACH'S NOTE

1. People will, more times than not, send more than one signal at a time. Above all, do not counter with a combination response. Separate their double or triple signals; then respond to each signal distinctly.
2. If your interactions are negative or not satisfying, you are either in the wrong place or you are missing signals. Quietly step back and take a new look. Express your confusion and ask for new signals or a review of the old ones.
3. Many people will be deaf, dumb, and blind to your signals. Just keep sending them; eventually they will get through. Be creative, improvise—but make sure you have their attention first.
4. You know when your signals are effective because your self-esteem goes up in direct proportion to your effective signals.
5. Signals are not the message—they are the medium. If you are driving down the street and the light signals green, it doesn't mean there are no other cars coming. You have to be willing to take a close look. Listen to and respond to signals but don't take the signals as the experience. They just get things started.

CHAPTER

·20·

How to Send and
Receive the Right Signals

I spend many hours teaching clients about the signals they are sending and teaching them how to read other people's signals. To learn to read Public Zone signals we often go out for walks. On day Shelly and I were out walking and we came upon a man crossing the street. He read the traffic signal correctly. And yet cars were streaming past him. Then he began to scream at the drivers. He was sure that he was right and yet he was putting himself into a losing situation. What he failed to notice was the traffic cop who was sending the drivers a hand signal to go.

A signal is the basic human connector. If you can send the right signals and respond correctly to the signal someone else is sending—you *connect.* And that connection makes it possible for you to stay in the right place. One study reports that people with the fewest social connections have two to four times the mortality rate of the well connected. It listed several ways people connect, to wit: 1) emotional concern (liking, loving, empathy), 2) instrumental aid (goods or services), 3) information (about the environment), or 4) appraisal (information relevant to self-evaluation).

If you don't know how to send and receive the full range of signals, your contacts go down. Desmond Morris in *The Pocket Guide to Man Watching* describes the similarity between human and animal signals. It is quite interesting that human beings consider themselves superior to animals while in fact animals communicate very well with each other—and with humans. Anyone who owns a cat can tell you that the cat not only lets you know what it wants but when and how. There is much to learn from a study of animal communication. You learn quickly that it is not enough for you to *mean* stop or go, your signal of stop or go must be understandable.

Here are the twelve basic signal groups I teach clients:

1. Public Signals
2. Social Signals
3. Personal Signals
4. Intimate Signals
5. Information Signals
6. Emotional Signals
7. Psychological Signals
8. Physical Signals
9. Success and Motivation Signals
10. Need and Want Signals
11. Respect and Recognition Signals
12. Sexual Signals

Learning to Use the Twelve Signals

The first four signals—public, social, personal, and intimate— are marker signals. They tell you what zone you are in.

Public Signals

These signals will help you make the Public Zone a place where you connect. Remember, in the Public Zone it is vital to make your intentions clear. And the only intentions appropriate for the Public Zone are friendly intentions. But how are other people going to know that? For many people the Public Zone is an unfriendly and frightening place. If you want to make a connection, you have to make sure you are clear, concise, open, and friendly. Here are some of the signals that will let other people know your intentions:

Offer brief but direct eye contact.
Maintain a friendly but assertive attitude.
Smile easily at people.

Talk about public events and situations to which you and the
   people you are with have equal access.
Pay attention to what is happening around you.
Be open to the novel and different.
Show courtesy.
Break the ice.

With all the signals you send and receive in the Public Zone, it
is vital to remember that this zone is a low-risk, high-access area.
If you want to be successful, just keep sending your signals. Eventually you will get very good at sending them and at receiving
the Public Zone signals others send you. When you feel more
comfortable there, you will realize that people are sending you
these signals all the time. They are often very discreet and covert.
If you give a gentle response to their signals you will find people
taking chances with you that they normally wouldn't take with a
stranger. Since you are a stranger with strangers, it is vital that
you *not* start sending personal or intimate signals.

Social Signals

Effective social signals *increase* the success of whatever activity is occurring. If you are at work, the signals are about
performance, motivation, positive criticism, and enthusiasm. If
you are at a party, your signals are friendly, outgoing, inquisitive,
activity oriented, directed toward others.

Whenever you are in the Social Zone, it is vital that you keep
the signals flowing. You are then like a lighthouse for other people. They can relate to you because of your steady stream of signals.

Any social signal requires a social signal in response for a connection to occur. The fastest way to break a social connection is
to give a personal, intimate, or public response to a social signal.
Social signals are about performance. They are not about another
person—they are about *what* is happening, not *who* is doing it.
Social signals connect you with the people you are sharing an
activity with. The easiest way for that connection to occur is for
you to concentrate on the activity. And most important, don't let
your social signals become charged with emotion or your own
importance.

Coach's Cues for Effective Social Signals

If someone invites you to do something—and you want to connect—respond with a definite yes or no.

If someone gives you a compliment—and you want to connect—respond by saying thank you and accepting the compliment.

If someone is complaining about work or a boss—and you want to connect—respond by asking what he or she could do differently. Your signal says, I am not going to get negative, but I'll listen to you for a while.

If someone is trying to do something new—and you want to connect—respond by offering encouragement.

If someone is doing something—and you want to connect—respond by giving praise.

COACH'S NOTE

In the Social Zone, things are bound to go wrong from time to time. When this happens, don't look for someone to blame—look for the little *mis*es. You can change a potentially negative situation into a positive one by simply saying: "Let's find out where we got our wires crossed." Remember—everyone thinks he knows what was said and what happened. And when something is going wrong there is an opportunity for you to take charge and turn a potentially negative situation into a positive one.

Personal Signals

Personal signals tell others how you are feeling and what you are thinking and not about what you are doing. Many people confuse their personal and social signals. They start talking about some event and before you know it, they are talking emotionally. Look out! Signal confusion. A personal signal requires a personal signal in response for a connection to occur.

You are sending or receiving a personal signal whenever you hear:

What I think is . . .

I got really upset about what happened.

I just don't know what to do.

My feelings got hurt.

When you hear a personal signal or notice one, and if you want to connect, make the shift and start sending your personal signals in return. If you don't want to connect, just be quiet and let the other person gracefully back out of the situation.

Intimate Signals

Intimate signals are signals about you and another person. You are in the Intimate Zone whenever you hear:

I feel so good about you and me.

I love you.

What do you think about me?

What are you feeling?

You really hurt my feelings.

Remember, intimate signals are about sharing. They are not about doing something or accomplishing something. You don't have to do anything except share. One of the most disappointing experiences is to send an intimate signal and not get a response. An intimate signal comes from the heart and is laced with vulnerability. Have the sensitivity to respond with care to the intimate signals of others.

Information Signals

An information signal is the basic unit of interaction in which facts, figures, and ideas are transmitted. Shelly was very good at sending and receiving information signals. That was one of the reasons for her success at work, since information signals are the key to success in the Public and Social Zones. *Someone who sends you an information signal needs to get an information signal back.* But to send and receive information correctly, you have to take the time to really understand the other person's information—not what you think they mean but what they actually mean. Moreover, many people take information personally. If the information they are receiving does not match the information they already possess, they don't take it in.

Giving and receiving teaches you just how different people are. Two people reading the same article construe it differently. And many people expect others to understand them no matter how they send information. That is a mistake. If you want to connect, then it is up to you to make sure your information is conveyed. This is the time to be specific, to be clear, and to be focused on getting the information across. When you are sending an information signal it is vital that you don't allow the information to become emotional. Sending or receiving information requires that you focus on the information.

Coach's Cues for Information Signals

Respond by repeating verbatim what was said and what you understood, before going on. For example, if a friend says to you, "Let's go to Chow Lin's Chinese, tomorrow at seven," respond first with "Chow Lin's, tomorrow at seven," and then "Of course, I'd love to" or whatever else you want to say. Double-check early and you won't have to work out the problems later on. This means setting your appointments, dates, and meetings and having everyone involved reconfirm, right then, exactly what was agreed upon.

If someone looks perplexed or inquisitive, or if it is clear that you and another are not communicating—and you want to connect—respond by asking directly if you can be of help. Don't wait for others to tell you they don't know something when it is important to you that they do. I witnessed a good example of this attitude at my daughter's school. On registration day, the school had volunteers wearing bright yellow T-shirts that read: ASK ME. It was a public event and they made it easy to get information. You can do the same for the people in your life you want to connect with. Take the initiative and find out.

If someone gives you a deadline—and you want to connect—here again, respond: "I hear you saying that the deadline you want is such and such. I agree with it" or "I can't make it."

If someone is not saying anything at all but not going away—and you want to connect—here again, respond by asking if you can help.

COACH'S EXERCISE

Think about what kind of information you grew up with. Did you learn to communicate information clearly and with great accuracy? Notice when you are *not* paying attention to the information signals other people are sending out. Then notice when others are not paying attention to the signals you are sending.

COACH'S NOTE

When you know that someone is sending information signals, it is a good indication that you are in either the Social or the Public Zone. Keep yourself clear as to what zone you are in so that you don't take any of the little *mis*es personally. When you are in the Intimate and Personal Zones, listen very carefully to the information someone sends you. The information is bound to be charged with emotion.

Emotional Signals

The connecting response to emotional signals is an acknowledgment of those feelings. When emotional signals are being sent, you are generally in the Personal and Intimate Zones. But you can be at a public event and send and receive emotional signals of joy, grief, or praise. Or if you are in the Social Zone and someone is sending an emotional signal of appreciation or praise, acknowledge it. Remember, if you are with someone who is sending you emotional signals and you want to connect, respond with your own feelings. You don't have to feel, or agree with, what someone else is feeling—but to be effective you need to *recognize* those feelings.

Men very often miss emotional signals entirely. They think that an emotional signal means there must be something to do or that the emotion should be stopped. The simple and effective response to an emotion is to express a confirming emotion. If something needs to be fixed or learned, that can be done once the emotion has subsided. When people send you emotional signals and you don't respond, they often withdraw. If you find people withdrawing from you, it just might be that you are missing their emotional signals.

Coach's Cues for Emotional Signals

If someone says:

"I feel that. . . ," respond, "I've felt that way myself" or "I can understand how you feel."

"I am sad (or mad, or glad)," respond, "I don't feel that way right now but I know what you feel."

"I just don't know what to do," respond, "I have had that happen to me many times and I understand."

"I just wish this hadn't happened," respond, "Lots of times these things happen and they make me feel terrible."

"I am really nervous," respond, "I get nervous in situations like that."

Once you know someone is sending an emotional signal, make sure you give emotional acknowledgment. *Nothing* feels better when someone is sending an emotional signal than to get an acknowledgment for it. This doesn't mean you have to become maudlin or overly emotional—a simple confirmation is enough.

Psychological Signals

Psychological signals are about a person's inner exploration and search for understanding into himself or herself. A psychological signal is self-revealing and requires a response of self-revelation if you want to make a connection. When someone is sending a psychological signal, listen carefully to what is being said. The person is not necessarily looking for advice. To connect, reveal something of yourself in return. It was very surprising for Shelly to discover how often people were sending her psychological signals and how frequently she misunderstood them. She discovered not only that psychological signals were important but that when she wanted to send those self-revealing signals herself, she didn't know how.

Coach's Cues for Psychological Signals

If someone says:

"I just don't understand what happened," respond, "Tell me; what did you think happened?"

"I keep making the same mistake over and over," respond, "I

have made the same kind of mistake. Let's talk about it and maybe we can learn why."

"I don't know what to do," respond, "When I don't know what to do, I feel insecure. It happens to all of us."

"I feel confused," respond, "I know exactly what confusion feels like. What does it feel like to you?"

"This is troubling me," respond, "I have been troubled lots of times and I have had a lot of practice working it through."

"I am upset by what happened," respond, "I know what you mean. But exactly what did happen?"

COACH'S NOTE

Psychological signals tell you you are in the Personal Zone. You have to get ready for making the Personal Zone connections if you want to continue going forward.

Physical Signals

Physical signals are the signals of touch and comfort, and of the human physical bond, and they require human touch in return. We often confuse physical signals with sexual signals. Physical signals are the basic dance of humanity. Shelly found that she was shy about sending physical signals, but as she practiced sending these signals she became more effective in all the different life zones. She was willing to stand closer to people, touch more, and take the risk of breaking the distance barrier between herself and the people in her life.

Coach's Cues for Physical Signals

Someone reaches out to hug you. Hug back and say something.

Someone is feeling down and withdrawn. Reach out and break through the loneliness with a touch.

Someone is feeling great. Hug and kiss them to let them know you support their good feeling.

Someone is having a hard time. Reach out and let them know you are there.

Someone greets you. Respond with a warm hug, a handshake, or a kiss.

COACH'S NOTE

Physical signals work well in all four zones. The more you let
yourself be naturally physical, the more confident you will be.
You don't have to wait to return a hug. You can initiate it.

Success and Motivation Signals

Shelly was great at sending and responding to success and
motivation signals. It means giving the support and encouragement necessary to keep trying, to strive for more, to overcome
the obstacles that keep us from reaching our goals.

Coach's Cues for Success and Motivation Signals

Someone is trying to learn something new and feels like quitting. Respond: "I know it is hard but remember what you want to
learn. Don't settle for not knowing what to do."

Someone is trying to get a new job and is worried about it.
Respond: "It's a game and you can play it like a game. Don't take
it personally."

Someone is trying to increase self-esteem by losing weight,
going to new places, or being more assertive. Respond: "It takes a
long time to win but I want you to know you have my support."

Success signals may seem trite until you need one yourself.
Learn to use them well and you'll become an expert connector.

COACH'S NOTE

Give success and motivation signals in all four zones. They are
the basis of many reward systems.

Need and Want Signals

If you can learn to send out your need and want signals clearly,
you are giving the people in your life an opportunity to become
more competent and powerful. People actually like to satisfy the
needs and wants of others when they can. A need is something
that is vital to your success and survival; a want is something that

gives you pleasure but is not necessary for your survival or success. When you signal someone else about what you need, you can't demand that they respond, know how to supply what you need, or be able to understand your signals right away. Your signal is the reference point for another person to address you.

Coach's Cues for Need and Want Signals

If someone says to you, "I want you to give me or get me . . ." and you are able to oblige, then do so. If you are not able to oblige, say, "I would love to but I am not able to right now." Give other people the recognition they need for their wants.

If people say, "I need. . . ," give them recognition for their needs. It doesn't matter if you can fill their needs or not. *What matters is giving the recognition and letting them know what you can do, or what you need to learn to fill their needs.* You don't have to know how to fill each need another person has; what you need to do is allow others to state their needs even when you cannot fill them.

COACH'S NOTE

People have needs and wants in all four zones. Your job is to find out what zone you are in so that your response to their signals is appropriate. If you are in the Public Zone, respond to their need with information; if you are in the Social Zone, respond to their need with participation; if you are in the Personal Zone, respond to their need with emotional understanding; and if you are in the Intimate Zone, your number-one response: love.

Respect and Recognition Signals

The politics of human communication is governed by two key signals: respect and recognition. If you can show respect for what others are saying, for their position and their experience, then you are learning to master the signals that will make your life better. Recognition of someone else is a vital aspect of respect. Recognition means listening to what others have to say. Respect and recognition mean you are no longer trying to be right all the time. When someone points out his way of doing something or his thought about something, take the time to listen. Giving others recognition does not imply that they are correct. It simply means you are taking the time to offer them a respectful hearing. Don't always insist on doing it your way—it is a sign of disrespect always to have to do it your way. Besides, we all know there is more than one way to do anything.

COACH'S NOTE

Respect and recognition signals are usually in short supply in all four zones. Make sure you pick up on others' signals and recognize when you need respect from others.

Sexual Signals

You are giving off sexual signals all the time to people of both sexes. The question you want to ask is, what kind of signals am I giving off?

Here are some of the basic sexual signals:

I am not sexual.

I am sexual.

I am sexual and mature.

I am sexual and immature.

When you are sexual and mature you are able to know your sexual place with both sexes. This means you know how you fit in with the same sex. For example, sexually potent and confident people read each other's sexual signals and feel comfortable with each other, while the sexually immature person feels uncomfortable with others of the same sex. The immature person shows this with arguments, excessive competitiveness, and fears. The sexually mature person is able to be physically warm with men and women in a nonsexual way, while the sexually immature person is often overtly sexual or asexual with the opposite sex and resistant to physical contact with the same sex.

When you are in sync, you send a positive sexual signal. On the other hand, insecurity sends a negative sexual message. To send strong sexual messages you must know what zone you are in and what message is appropriate for that zone. If you are in the Public Zone, then a mild but direct flirtation is a strong signal. If you are in the Social Zone, then direct eye contact, physical closeness, and touching are strong sexual signals. In the Personal Zone, expressing your sexual arousal and your pleasure is a strong sexual signal. And in the Intimate Zone, expressing concern and care for the other's pleasure is a strong sexual signal. When you want to be sexual, take control over the signals you send. The stronger your sexual signals, the stronger the responses you will get in return.

There are many other signals to send and to pick up on, but these *twelve basic signals* are so predominant that if you learn to recognize when someone is sending them and to respond effectively you will find the right place and the right time easily.

Remember, signals are the basic connectors. If there is no connection, there can be no communication or understanding.

How Do You Know You Are Sending the Right Signals?

When you are sending the right signals, you can feel it. You are in sync with the other person; you are in step with each other. It doesn't matter if the two of you are fighting, negotiating, making love, or having tea—if your signals are right, you are with each other. The depth of your togetherness is determined by the zone you are in.

We are ready to go to the final section. Why don't you take a little break right now and think about the signals you send and the signals you receive.

COACH'S NOTE

---

1. In the Public Zone your signals are the right ones when you make that momentary connection, you have a sense of orientation and freedom, and you know what is happening around you.
2. In the Social Zone you know your signals are the right ones when you find yourself actively doing something. If you say, "Let's go play tennis," and then find yourself on the court by yourself, your signals aren't working right.
3. In the Personal Zone you know you are sending the right signals because you feel vulnerable. You are open to the people

you are with and they are open to you. The right signals let others know you are paying attention to their feelings, sensitivity, thoughts. If you really pay attention and the other person doesn't, then you must realize the situation isn't really personal. In the Personal Zone, there is back and forth, and a natural ebb and flow.

4. You know your Intimate Zone signals are correct because you feel accepted by the person you are with and that person lets you know he or she feels accepted.

Section Seven

THE FOUR STEPS

CHAPTER

·21·

The Life-Athlete's
Checklist

By now you ought to have some tools for putting yourself into sync and should find that you feel more
effective. What you have learned is how to answer the four simple questions I proposed in the introduction:

QUESTION ONE: Where are you right now?
QUESTION TWO: What are your needs?
QUESTION THREE: What images are you using?
QUESTION FOUR: What signals are you sending and what signals
   are you receiving?

These four questions are the life-athlete's checklist. Any professional makes sure he or she has the basics taken care of before
starting action. The tennis player checks rackets, tennis shoes,
light, wind, and court conditions. The race-car driver checks
tires, fuel, and track conditions. The underwater diver checks
oxygen, gauges, and water temperature and currents. For a professional, going over checklists has become a habit. Most often
you won't even notice professionals going through their checklists. But they do.
   In life most people don't use checklists. They wade into life,
which is much more dangerous than driving a car or flying a
plane, without a checklist. They don't know what to do when
something goes wrong or, when something is going right, how to
keep it going. If you use this life-athlete's checklist anytime you

feel good or bad, you are going to become a professional life-athlete. The greatest difference between a professional athlete and an amateur is consistency. On any given day an amateur may give a great performance. But next time the amateur will make silly mistakes that lead to failure. The professional is consistently good. And the champion is good under pressure.

One of my clients recently asked me if she now would have to use these questions for the rest of her life. I asked her if each time she got into her car she checked the gas, the warning lights, and where she was going. She said yes. I said, "Then that is the answer. Do for your life what you do for your car—use your checklist."

The great basketball coach John Wooden, who won ten national basketball titles at UCLA, used to say that his teams won not by being that much better than the other teams but by being good when others let down and made mistakes. Professionals don't make as many mistakes as amateurs because they use their checklists. Could it be that simple? The answer is an unqualified YES. Remember, your questions prepare you for taking action by letting you know where you are, what you need, what image you are using, what signal you are sending. As you ask your questions, you are going to find yourself making decisions about what you want to do. And with each decision you learn more about how to play the game of life. If you use your questions, you will find yourself winning more, but you need to make that extra effort. I want you to get to the point where you ask and answer the four questions automatically. As you do, you will find yourself more successful in any action you take because you will eliminate your most common mistakes by going through your checklist. Don't wait to use it until you are having a problem—use it to increase your chances for success.

This doesn't mean you are always going to get what you want, or that you are going to win. It simply means that you are going to deal effectively with any situation. The more you use this powerful new tool, the more competent you become. You can use it to make a bad situation better. Or to keep a situation going. When we feel good, we usually hold our breaths and hope that our luck will hold. Instead, we should be saying "What's the formula? How did I get here? I got here through actions I took." And when we are feeling bad, we should say the same thing: "I got here through the actions I took. The results are not mysterious."

When you answer the first question—"Where am I right now?"—you are discovering the right zone. Once you know *where* you are, you are ready to act. And by asking the second question—"What are my needs?"—you turn on your human machine. When you know what you need, your personality system is preparing to take the right action, the action that satisfies your need. Think about it. If you know what life zone you are in and what you need, action opportunities become obvious. The specific kind of action you take is determined by the answer to the third question: "What images am I using?" When *where* you are and what you *need* are clear, you know that *image* is appropriate for that time and place. You're then ready for the fourth question: "What signals am I sending and receiving?" It is your self that will send and receive the signals you will use to determine what to do. Your answers to these questions make it possible for you to maximize the situation that you are in and to be at your best.

There will be times when the stress in your life will make answering seem impossible. But it is in those situations that you can actually minimize your stress by asking the four questions. When you start to stumble, the questions enable you to catch yourself sooner, and stop yourself before your mistakes get out of control. Instead of getting involved with what you are doing wrong, you are able to stay focused on finding the right place, the right need, and the right signal. As a life-athlete you use problems as cues to go back to the foundation of your success—the four questions.

In this book you have learned how to change. *And human change is the central focus of this book.* I have found that *when people know they can change,* problems give way to solutions, despair gives way to hope, and stagnation gives way to growth. Just by reading this book you have changed. It doesn't matter how small may be the change you have made. Was it understanding some new information? Did you become aware of one of your out-of-date images? Did you rediscover "you at your best"? It doesn't matter how small you think your change was. You learned something and we can build on that learning. Remember, we are not getting ready for a test—we are slowly preparing you for the rest of your life. Give yourself a reward for the change you have made. *Change is contagious.* Get a little change started and before you know it you will be caught up in a wave of change.

Shelly changed. The first major change Shelly went through was in attitude. She developed the new attitude of playing life like a game.

The new attitude allowed her to try, to explore, to do what was new and different, to think new thoughts and try new options, to feel new feelings and to allow her self to guide her life. Mistakes were no longer reasons to get depressed or to blame someone else. Mistakes became her cues for going back to her checklist of the four questions.

Almost eighteen months to the day after Shelly first came to see me, what she told me illustrated the change she had made. I knew by what she said that her self was in control. She sat down and began talking in a slow but easy-to-listen-to voice.

"Something has happened to me. I didn't really notice it until about ten days ago. And then I realized I just wasn't the same. I have control of my life. I know that may seem vague, but that is exactly what it feels like. It really hit me the other day. A series of extremely successful things had happened at work and I was feeling great. I was at the office and then around four-thirty I went home. I fixed dinner for the kids and helped them with their homework. Randy came home around seven-thirty from his office and we all visited. He and I went upstairs and showered together. We were just talking, but I felt close to him. It was as if we had passed through some barrier we didn't even know existed. And then, while I fixed my hair and put on my makeup, Randy finished helping the kids with their homework. I kissed them goodnight and told them to be in bed by ten-thirty. We went to dinner, and got home around eleven-forty-five. At dinner there weren't the usual spats and hurts, fits and starts. We were connected and it seemed easy. When we got home we got into bed and made love. It was about pleasure and tenderness and caring. Sex was the vehicle. We fell asleep and then we started the next day over again. Except it wasn't life as usual. I still had this feeling of control, as if I had this inner compass to guide me. It is the same feeling I have when I feel just right; when I know what to say, and do, and my emotions are under my control."

What had happened to Shelly? She had done more than get over her problems. She had developed and was using the power to be in the right place at the right time.

When we started this book I told you I was a coach. The game I coach is the game of life. But to live life effectively and fully requires you to play it like a game. What had happened to Shelly was that she had learned to play the game of life. She knew the rules, the zones, and the signals. She knew her needs, her rewards, and her self. Shelly was taking new actions and experiencing new freedoms. Shelly was not concerned only with Shelly, she was concerned with life, the people in it, and how to live as fully as possible. The attitude Shelly developed you already know about because you learned it in Chapter One.

To play the game of life you have to let go, to allow yourself to trust life. If you play, life teaches you to fill your needs and the needs of those you are with. *The game of life is a way of change in a changing world.* The game is about life itself.

If you can trust change, you can give up the illusion of certainty. Images are certain about certainty. Your images are convinced they know what is real, concrete, and true because they are tapes or programs. They begin and end. The self is willing to live with uncertainty.

Many people take what they don't know, what feels uncomfortable, or what they can't do as a reason to quit, to stop playing, to follow the lead of their images, to be certain. What Shelly didn't know, couldn't do, or felt uncomfortable with were no longer objects of fear. She had changed them into opportunities and challenges. *She no longer backed away from the unknown.* People become so worried that the outcome they are looking for won't match their expectations that they avoid doing anything except what they know they can already do. They don't remember that they are remembering. They forget they *aren't* making choices but are simply playing the tapes they have stored in their memories. They forget that they have choices. They mistake the familiarity of images for the satisfaction of taking action in the unknown, where out-of-date images are useless.

COACH'S NOTE

At any moment. In any situation. You have choice.

The game of life is played in the unknown. Most games have a beginning, middle, and end. The game of life doesn't. You discover as you play the game of life that being in sync is a phenomenon of here and now. This is all that we really have and if we learn to deal with the here and now, then we have control. *And as you play each moment the best you can, being in sync brings you one opportunity after another.* The more you play the more you realize that many of your fears are paper tigers or trolls under bridges, created by your out-of-date images, which divert your self from taking control. And as you play you find a new intensity, an intensity that makes life worth living. It is that intensity that is the sweetness of life. It enlivens and heals. It is the stuff of miracles. This new intensity is the reason for living.

The greatest of athletic champions play to attain that intensity through their sport. This intensity, which is created by your own action, is the forge of human experience. You are no longer removed from life; you are in it, and you are making it happen. The past no longer directs you. Instead, you are at your best in the present striving for the future. Bill Russell, one of the greatest athletes of all time, wrote:

Every so often a Celtic game would heat up so that it became more than a physical or even a mental game, and would be magical. That feeling is difficult to describe. . . . When it happened I could feel myself rise to a new level. . . . It would surround not only me and the other Celtics but also the players on the other team, and even the referees. To me, the key was that both teams had to be playing at their peaks, and they had to be competitive. . . . The feeling would spread to the other guys, and we'd all levitate. Then the game would just take off, and there'd be a natural ebb and flow. . . . The game would be in a white heat of competition and I wouldn't feel competitive. . . . It was almost like we were playing in slow motion. . . . I could almost sense how the next play would develop. . . .

What happens in those special times to those athletes is an American version of the experiences of enlightenment, satori, and freedom from images. By being at their best they were momentarily swept up beyond the image of playing basketball, baseball, tennis, golf—they were dancing with life itself. They had in those rare moments the experience of self in action. You can have this feeling for longer than a few precious moments.

This experience of feeling is the reason people write, paint, research, live life with commitment, and struggle against odds. It is the direct route to what life has to offer. Bill Russell found that it wasn't winning that motivated him but that feeling. When you play the game of life—each problem, each crisis, each celebration becomes part of life—you no longer have to react to the eruptions as if they weren't supposed to be there. In the game of life the celebration comes every day from playing moment by moment with what is. You stop getting upset because life isn't what you think it ought to be. Instead, you play life as it presents itself to you. You are playing the most complex, most interesting, and most rewarding game you will ever play. The game of life is not about the final score but the playing. Your self has the potential to play your life with greatness. You don't have to discover a new continent, cure cancer, or make the winning touchdown. You win at the game of life by living the life you have to its fullest. The game is played with courage, intensity, goodwill, honesty, and enthusiasm. In this game you are important but not the center of attention.

No one else—no doctor, no coach, no lover or spouse—can ultimately play your game for you. However, while you must play, you do not play alone. There are other players in the game of life. Although what you experience—both your failures and your successes—may be unique, it can be shared with others. You are not the only person to think the thought that seems so embarrassing, so profound, or so terrible. You are not the only person who has felt the feelings of rage or hurt, love, guilt, or despair. We are similar to each other. We have come from the same blood, we have the same bones, and we have the same hearts.

Shelly found that to be successful, and to find happiness, she had to take new action. This is what all my successful clients do, what successful businesses do, and what successful players in the game of life do. They take new action. They don't play safe. Playing means you change. You change to play life as it is, not as you wish it to be. And you play life in the here and now. And it is in playing life that you find the freedom to be.

Covert Bailey in his book *Fit or Fat* teaches one key to successful weight loss. To lose weight a person must change his or her metabolic system from anaerobic to aerobic. The anaerobic system does not utilize oxygen efficiently and tends to burn and store sugars. No matter how much you try to diet, losing weight is difficult, and the weight you do lose is almost never kept off. In his book Bailey teaches you to change your system to one that is aerobic or oxygen-burning, which is also a fat-burning system. It may take six months of exercise for twelve to twenty minutes three to four times a week at a "training" level to create your aerobic system. But once you have changed your system you are able to lose weight and keep it off.

Becoming aerobic takes time and there is no miracle five-day crash course. The image wants to lose the five pounds fast. The self is willing to change. It is intellectually so much easier to list the foods you shouldn't eat than to discover that you must take new action. But once you change your system, the details (the foods, the problems, the past history) are easy to deal with. This is how the game of life works.

Earlier I talked about the difference between going to the doctor's office and to the coach on the playing field. If you go to the doctor you expect him to do something or give you something to provide a permanent cure. But when you go to the coach, what you are learning is only the beginning. In the game of life you change through *your* action and you know that if you stop taking action the old problems will reappear.

As you learn to play the game of life, you are going to go through four different steps. But we are never just at Step Two or Step Four. It is that fine tuning from step to step that lets you win. And even when you have reached Step Four there will be times when you find yourself back at Step Two. Don't despair. It is all part of the game. No one stars. Life is the center attraction. We are just the players. So play. Let's go to the next chapter and find out about the first step.

CHAPTER

·22·

Taking Control

I have noticed over the years that change takes place in four distinct steps. The first step occurs when a person decides to take control, the second step when a person begins to experience personal power, the third step when a person starts performing at higher levels, and finally, the fourth step when a person achieves a state of imagelessness. Each step leads to the next. You may find yourself going from Step Three back to Step One but don't worry about it. The steps are there to guide you, not rule you. Let's find out about Step One.

Step One: Taking Control

Wouldn't it be nice to have control? To be the one who has the say-so, the boss? There is no place and no person outside yourself over which you can have total control. But with yourself at each moment you can have control. Control does not mean moment-to-moment, action-to-action, feeling-to-feeling. Control is more like learning to sail a great ship. You can put yourself in a position to take maximum advantage of the winds. You can travel to exotic places. You can avoid the reefs. But control does not mean you never make a mistake, that bad things don't happen, or that you are better than the next person.

Learning to take control is entirely your affair. When you take control, you will feel like yourself and nothing can take that feeling and power away from you. How do you begin? You make a decision, the decision to take control. Once you make this decision you have changed the rules of your life. You no longer *have to* feel how you are feeling or do what you are doing. When you decide to take control, you have choice. What is doesn't have to be any longer than you want it to be. The first step is just the beginning, because taking control means learning new mechanisms for thinking, feeling, and behavior.

What I Am Doing Isn't Working

Taking control starts by admitting that what you are doing is not working. And what you are doing isn't working if you don't have the sense of "you at your best." It takes self-esteem to admit you are losing the way you are playing. *Losing means you are not playing up to your potential.* Losing also means that the way you are doing things, how you react emotionally, the patterns you have in your life, are not satisfying your needs. Here is a coaching question I use all the time: "Is what you are doing satisfying your needs?" When you answer, you are taking control. It doesn't matter what anyone else sees or thinks about you. You are the one who knows you aren't living at your potential. Let's use this checklist to find out if you are at Step One. Check the statements that are true for you.

Step One Checklist

1. Your relationships are repetitive. No matter how they start they always seem to wind up in the same place____
2. Certain words, situations, or people just seem to press your reaction buttons____
3. You spend more time getting over feeling bad than enjoying feeling good____
4. You get angry easily____
5. You frequently confuse the different life zones____
6. You have overreactions or underreactions, which hamper your effectiveness____
7. It is easy for you to blame other people____
8. You take misunderstandings, miscommunications, and misperceptions personally____

9. You are easily intimidated by others____
10. You keep thinking that you will take better care of yourself tomorrow ____
11. You have a chronic weight, smoking, or drinking problem ____
12. You can't find in adulthood the real pleasure that you once knew as a child ____
13. There is more miscommunication, misunderstanding, and misperception in your life than you would like____
14. You think you are right but often feel bad____
15. You think most of your problems are caused by other people____
16. You think there is "something" wrong with you____
17. You don't use "you at your best" as your daily reference point____
18. You have a drug problem (I want to put special emphasis on this point because millions of people have problems with prescribed drugs as well as with illicit drugs.)____
19. You are lonely____
20. You get hurt too often____

This checklist isn't like any of the other learning tests you have taken in this book because a single check means that you are at Step One. *Each item on the list represents a different way in which your out-of-date images are keeping you from taking control.*

Taking Control

Everyone has been or will be again at Step One. At Step One the self is controlled and trapped by the images. The person who has never taken the time or had the opportunity to think about his or her life is usually at Step One, but it can happen to the strongest person when the stress in his or her life becomes too great. In our society we judge things predominantly by their market value and not their inner worth. A person can be viewed as successful in the world and still be at Step One because of his or her lack of inner satisfaction. Let me give you an example.

One of my clients was an internationally known and respected photographer. He came to me because he was having a problem with his son. I was able to help him solve that problem, but he continued to see me.

One day he came in and slumped in the chair. It had finally happened. He realized just how unhappy he was. Not with his work but with himself. He slowly started to change. Because of the work we had done with his son, he saw just how trapped he had become by his out-of-date images. He had been taking care of his mother and four younger brothers since he was twelve years old. He had never asked "What do I need?" It was a difficult step for him to take, to admit that taking care of other people was no longer rewarding for him.

When he asked himself "What do I need?" he found more deprivation and emptiness than he had ever thought possible. He cried for the first time in thirty years, just thinking about how hard he had worked as a boy trying to take care of the family. He had carried this burden with him most of his life, a burden he never felt up to, the feeling that he was faking it, getting by. And in many ways he was. He was pretending to be the father and provider when he was just a boy. The more he learned about his needs, the fuller he became. He learned that as he took care of himself, he had much more to offer others. He renewed his life through change.

At Step One the outside world is filtered through the images. And whatever the self needs must first pass through the image wall. Your out-of-date images at Step One are like different pairs of glasses. They distort what comes in and what goes out. At Step One you are suffering from image distortion. This distortion includes the information you are using and the feelings you have and the thoughts you think.

Periodically, the self will break out but the out-of-date images have it, for all intents and purposes, trapped. The needs, actions, and rewards of the self are filtered out and distorted by the images that surround it. The images never go beyond the emotional frontier (beyond what they know or can feel). The signals you send and how you understand the signals from others are also distorted by your out-of-date images. You are trapped in an image vacuum. How do you know you are trapped? How do you know what is the image and what isn't? You can find out by asking "Am I having my needs met?" If your needs aren't being met, you are at Step One where "image to image" and "problem to problem" interact. An image will not see people as they are, for who they are. An image will keep trying to get from someone what it wants without regard for what that person is. This is the condition we frequently experience with the other people in our lives. We are surrounded not only by our own images but by their images. It is no wonder we have so much miscommunication, misperception, and misunderstanding.

COACH'S TIME OUT

Take a chance, right now, and ask yourself if your needs really are being met. And then watch how your images try to deny the truth. Your images will give you explanations to replace the truth. They will blame others, run away from the insight, or express hope for the future—but the image cannot stay in the here and now. You know when your needs aren't being met because you don't feel good. You feel like a victim.

Each image performs a set routine. Anything beyond the routine is the emotional frontier to the image. You are trapped by your out-of-date images because at the point where the image would have to cross the emotional frontier to satisfy your needs by doing something new and different, it stops, quits, or diverts you. This becomes your "failure point." It really isn't *your* failure point—it is the limit of the out-of-date image. Instead of crossing the emotional frontier, the image will start a fight or stop feeling good or find something wrong. *Your problems are cues that your images have you trapped.*

COACH'S EXERCISE

List three of your major problems.

1. _____

2. _____

3. _____

Now think about which image is involved with which problem. You can use your problems as springboards to guide you to un-covering the hidden image control.

Images keep control by sending out signals to the images of other people. If one of your images is "victim," you find someone whose image is "victimizer." If your image is "giver," then you find someone who is a "taker." If your image is "disappointed," then you find a "disappointer." You become Samson calling out for your Delilah.

At Step One people are relating out-of-date image to out-of-date image, as if each has an image wheel of fortune. They spin and someone else spins. If you match images—Prince Charming to Cinderella, helpless to helper, beauty to beauty, then you have a relationship. It may not be a relationship that satisfies your needs, but it certainly will give your image a stage on which to do its thing. An out-of-date image is always in the same play re-gardless of who the other players are. You become Eve hunting for the serpent. Once failure is complete, the out-of-date image acts like the "innocent victim": "Gee, what happened?" or "I was just following orders."

It is astonishing how we all believe our images. We are certain that the other people must be in the wrong, as if it were the first time anything like this had happened. The image tries to deny the reality of how repetitive it is, but once you get to the end of its play you find you have to start all over again. This is why you see people getting divorced and then marrying someone who is just like the person they divorced. Remember, the out-of-date image isn't looking out for your welfare but for the welfare of the self it knew when you created it. The out-of-date image doesn't know you have changed.

I want you to use your out-of-date images as cues to break out of your image prison. Every time you find yourself getting ready to use an out-of-date image, stop and take a good look at it. Then ask yourself this simple question: Is what I am doing really going to fill my need?

The better you get at noticing when you are using an out-of-date image, the less you will unconsciously reinforce it. Let me give you an example. One of my clients was a superb trial lawyer. He was known for his searing cross-examinations. In his personal life the image of "lawyer" would often take control and he would wind up accusing his wife of everything from forgetting to pick up the laundry to not appreciating it when he cooked dinner. With coaching he learned to use his accusations as a cue that his lawyer image was getting out of control. He had a lot of false starts in learning to change but eventually he succeeded.

Remember, you don't have to do something dramatic to make a change. You initiate change just by noticing. If you try to change too fast or push too hard, your personality takes it as a threat and gets defensive. Right now you probably don't have much control over your out-of-date images and you don't notice them until after they've acted in your behalf. Pretty soon you will find yourself noticing and changing your out-of-date-image behaviors before they get started. And then you have taken yourself beyond the control of your images.

At Step One the action you take in the world is through images. *You wind up doing, feeling, thinking, and needing what your images tell you is appropriate.* What this means is that each of your images is convinced that it knows how to run your life. Even if running your life means ruining it. If your "victim" image is in control, then you have a victim pattern.

Sam was a victim. He would idolize the women he dated. He put them on a pedestal. He never let them know what he needed. And slowly the women got the message. They started believing their own press clippings. They started to treat Sam as if he wasn't worth very much. And then, sure as the sun rises, Sam would start to feel neglected. He would blow up every six months and demand more attention. The women would get angry and fight back, accusing Sam of changing the rules, since he had told them he didn't need anything. By the time he was ending his fourth divorce, you might think that Sam would have figured it out. He hadn't. His victim image was in control. It took Sam a while but he finally started taking control over his victim pattern.

Judy's "controller" image was in charge of her life. She saw everything as if it needed to be controlled. She had the cockroaches in her apartment marching in formation. She couldn't figure out why she had to drink so much to relax. It took Judy a while to figure it out but she started to realize she was being controlled by her controller image.

At Step One the self is being bounced like a Ping-Pong ball between the out-of-date images. At one moment you are the victim and the next the angry crusader. Your self doesn't know what you need or how to get your needs filled. The images are in control.

At Step One your life gets into a familiar routine of endless ups and downs with a depressingly familiar regularity. If you examine your cycle you see that what you call your high points are high only because you are getting over your low points. You spend more time working on getting over feeling bad than you do feeling good. *It is only by changing the personality system that sustained success is possible.* The change we are making is from the image-control system to the self-control system. When the self is in control you feel good. It doesn't mean you are always happy, but it does mean you have a positive and energetic attitude about your life.

COACH'S NOTES

Think about how difficult it would be to have a relationship at Step One, with each person's images spinning like two "wheels of fortune." You'd have to coordinate your cycles. When you were high, the other person might be low. Conflict at Step One is inevitable.

Think about how much business is run at Step One. If most people in the company are controlled by their images, then they aren't able to give their attention to their work. They spend time trying to get out of their doldrums rather than feeling the best they can.

COACH'S EXERCISE

1. What are your chances of being in sync with your cycle?
2. What are your chances of reading and sending the correct signals?

Face it. We have all been through our cycles so frequently that it just might feel good to admit it. We act according to the dictates of our out-of-date images. *When you control your cycle, you know when you peak and for how long you peak and your probability of winning in the game of life goes up.* When you don't have control, it becomes very difficult to develop an accurate sense of timing because you don't know when you will be up or down. *You are consistently inconsistent.* Did you ever wonder how we make sense out of our inconsistency? We use belief systems.

COACH'S TIME-OUT: HOW TO GET OUT OF STEP ONE

You already know. You learned how in the chapters on the right place. Remember what you learned about the Four Life Zones—they are the key to getting out of Step One. If you know what zone you are in, you have begun breaking out of the image trap. One of the ways out-of-date images keep you trapped is through *zone confusion.* You can counter zone confusion by really concentrating on *where* you are. But I think you already know how to do this. Knowing *where* you are makes it possible for you to take Step Two.

COACH'S NOTES

1. When you are in sync, you can take action and you have choice. Choice is what scares us but it is choice that makes us human beings. It is choice that frees us from the inner god and inner tyrant—memory. You can choose. And when you choose you have power.
2. When you are in sync, your past (what happened to you) has become your past, and your present becomes this moment. Most people live between the past and the present while longing for the future. The future can only emerge from the present.
3. You can gain understanding from your past but it is positive action in the present that leads to knowledge, satisfaction, and contentment.

4. When you make the most of each situation you are in, you are
preparing the way for your future. And when you don't, you
are perpetuating your past. By making the most of each situation, you are learning, growing, and getting everything you
can from the situation and are then able to do the next thing
that comes along.

Let's go on to Step Two now and see what happens when you
break out of your image traps.

·23·

Personal Power

If you walk into the precincts of any major corporation, you know very quickly where the power is. In any city there are power centers. And each country has its power capital. But the real power in life is personal power. While you may not be able to do anything about nuclear war or Alzheimer's disease, you do have the power to do something about your life and the lives of those people you interact with. But how? You find personal power by taking little steps and making small changes. And there comes a time when all the little changes add up, when all the little steps have taken you farther than you thought, and then—it dawns on you—you have changed. You just know it. You have changed. You are no longer the way you used to be. Maybe for the first time in your life you know change is possible. It is nothing less than a rebirth of your self.

During the course of your adult life you will be reborn time and time again. This rebirth of your self from the cocoon of your images is a display of your power. You are now different from the way you used to be. You are no longer trapped. This process will occur over and over in your life. Even your best and most effective images will one day no longer be satisfying and you will need to leave them behind.

Tatum never thought she could accept herself. She had failed in just about everything she had ever done. Tatum was a "trust fund baby." She never had to work; she never had to do anything. What she did do was fail. She failed in relationships, she failed at sports, she failed at finishing the book she had started. When she first came to see me I was surprised at how such an intelligent and beautiful woman could be so unhappy. She was eager to admit that she was a failure. What she resisted was telling me about her best. We started with her failure attitude. And then we moved on to learning about the life zones, and then about what she needed. We took her images on later. At each step "failure" was foremost in her mind. I just kept her moving forward, learning new concepts, thinking about what was happening to her, and trying small new steps. Then, like noticing something beautiful you own but haven't paid attention to before, Tatum noticed she had changed. It wasn't the way she had expected it to be. There was no *big* change. All the little changes added up. She knew she wasn't going to fail because for the first time she knew she wasn't going to quit. Tatum's adult self was being born.

When you experience the difference between being trapped by your images and the exhilaration of being reborn as an adult, you aren't suddenly free of all your old habits and attitudes. What is different is that your habits, attitudes, and beliefs don't control you the way they used to. And you won't get depressed the way you used to. Why? You stop before a problem goes too far and you use your mistakes as learning tools.

When you don't fall so far down, you have more time and energy to satisfy the needs of your self. You feel vulnerable because you are leaving the protective ignorance of the images. Step Two is difficult because it is a transition. You are changing from being a child-adult to being an adult-adult. At Step Two you are not yet an adult and yet no longer a child. But you are surely on your way.

Step Two Checklist

1. Some days you feel great and then you lose it for no apparent reason _____
2. You have trouble sustaining your motivation _____
3. You have important insights about your life and then you forget what they were _____
4. You know how you want to be with someone and then just can't carry it off _____

5. You have a feeling inside yourself of what you want but you can't seem to make it happen in your life_____
6. You start to recognize your ineffective patterns but can't change _____
7. You begin to act differently but then you drift back into your old behavior_____
8. You try new things but get embarrassed when you do _____
9. You realize other people are trying to put you into their image plays _____
10. You know that change is happening within you even if you can't sustain it_____
11. You get sad instead of depressed_____
12. You have a feeling that you are changing_____

If you checked any item here it means you are at Step Two. Learn from each of the questions and then use them all as hints for breaking out of your image traps.

At Step Two your images are no longer containing the self. The self is getting stronger and the images no longer filter and distort the information from the world. Once this happens your self gets stronger and stronger with each day. The image can't stop your self once it is getting and giving clearer information.

At Step Two your perception of the emotional frontier—what is unknown, scary, and difficult to do—is changing. You begin to realize that it was your out-of-date images that feared the emotional frontier, and as your images lose control, the emotional frontier gets smaller. Your self enjoys the unknown. The self feels good in the unknown because it begins exploring its potential. Like a runner stretching out his or her muscles, the self begin to work at its potential in the unknown.

At Step Two you have those moments when you are "you at your best" and you connect with another person self to self. But then the images regain control. The stronger the self gets, the more it receives signals directly from the world and the more effectively it responds. You are starting to take control but you still don't know how to keep it.

COACH'S NOTE

Just think for a minute. If you get and give clear information to the world, you know what people are really saying to you and you can make sure they know what you have to say. The opportunities are vast.

When the self breaks the image trap it is able to send stronger signals to the world because its signals are not being filtered through or blocked by the images. You start to notice at Step Two that "things" are changing in your life. People seem friendlier and getting what you want seems easier. A real key to knowing you are at Step Two is that you realize just how much time you have been wasting. You no longer have time for your image routines or the image routines of anyone else.

For Shelly, being at Step Two meant she could identify those situations and places in which she would normally quit or let an image take over.

COACH'S EXERCISE: HOW TO TAKE STEP TWO

Under special circumstances—a war, a crisis, a religious experience—or being with someone who has a strong self that connects easily to your self, you can temporarily move from Step One to Step Two. But as the crisis ends or the special person goes away or makes a mistake, the images return with a vengeance and retake control.

There is another way to Step Two and you already know it. It is learning to identify your images and find out if they are filling your needs. Let me give you an example. Missy could never distinguish among the four zones. Whenever her work was going well she felt wonderful, but with the smallest rejection or disapproval from her boss she would feel hurt and be unable to work. Missy discovered she was taking the Social Zone too personally. I had her watch baseball games (which she hated) to discover how to stop taking her strikeouts at work personally. She came back after a long weekend of baseball and said, "I couldn't believe those baseball players; they get up there in front of thousands and thousands of people and strike out. And then two innings later they get a hit." She had learned about being in sync.

As Shelly learned about her own personal synchrony, her cycle began to take on a new look. She was no longer dropping to her old familiar lows. She was spending far more time feeling good. That is another key to knowing you are at Step Two. You feel good more of the time. It is not that you are happy; instead, it is that positive Player Attitude again. You feel competent and know that you will do what it takes to find and sustain your own happiness. Shelly was learning to stay in the game of life. The probability of her winning had gone up dramatically because she was no longer a victim of her own cycle. She was sending clearer signals about what her needs were and she was reading other people's signals more effectively. What used to cause her pain, what used to be the time where she emotionally quit or became psychologically confused, were no longer the same.

Jackie knew she had taken Step Two when her husband came home late one night and for the first time in ten years she wasn't angry. She knew he had been working and her "victim" image didn't take over. She fixed him dinner and they talked. He kept wondering when she was going to start with her victim routine, but she never did. Jackie had taken the second step. She knew when her victim image was trying to take control and she stopped it.

To take the second step you muster your courage to go through what is uncomfortable and unfamiliar. For many people it means reining in their anger, or breaking their depression, but for all of us it means taking control over our out-of-date images. This courage that you have comes from your self. If you listen to your self, to what it needs, then you find that you are willing to do things that normally would have frightened you. As you take these new steps, your images will use *expectations* to fight against your self's taking control.

Changing Expectations

Expectations come from one of the three conditions (survival, adaptive, growth) we grew up in. A survival condition exists if your basic needs are not being met. You have to struggle to get the food, shelter, care, and love you need. You are also in a survival condition if there is violence and physical or psychological danger over which you don't have control or which is constant. If you grew up in a survival condition, you *expect* to live with deprivation and frustration. An adaptive condition is one that takes care of your basic survival needs but only a few of your needs for growth, stimulation, and self-to-self contact. If you grew up in an adaptive condition you *expect* never to be at your best. A growth condition exists when your needs for growth, stimulation, and self-to-self contact are at least partially filled. If you grew up in a growth condition you *expect* success and happiness.

One of my clients from a very deprived past developed an image of "a disappointed person." No matter what happened, he expected to be disappointed.

He recalled developing the image and the expectations during a particularly painful time in his early childhood, when his mother was in a major depression. Each day before the depression he would come home excited and eager to see her. And then as her depression worsened, she would sit by the window absently staring out. The discrepancy between his expectations and his home life was too great. His self took care of the problem—it created the "disappointed" image. He used to say, "If I don't want it that much, then it won't hurt if I don't get it." The disappointed image didn't expect to be excited. It expected disappointment. *There was no longer a discrepancy between his expectations and reality.* He grew older but the child-image remained. That child-image had been effective once, but as an adult his personality was stifled by the "disappointed" image.

As you take Step Two and the more you separate from your past, the more you have to face just what needs your self never had filled in childhood. You come to understand that your past was incomplete and that you adapted to it by changing yourself. One client had a history of suicide attempts. He kept trying to hurt himself. As he reached Step Two he had the insight that he had been hurt in his past, and now in his present he kept hurting himself to avoid knowing that the hurt had already happened. He kept denying what had actually occurred. Each image you have is an adaptive response to an environment you have gone through in your life. As you take control over the images, you begin to understand that you are not the image—you created the image in response to what was happening to you. It doesn't mean that there is something wrong with you.

Just think about it—the images of depressed, victim, helpless, no good, stupid, shy, afraid were all something you learned. They worked to help you survive at one time in your life. You can now see them for what they are—relics of your past. As you take control over your images you realize how much time you have lost by being trapped in your images. It is a painful and yet exciting realization. *At Step Two you know your childhood needs will never be filled.* And for many people there is a period of intense anger. They don't want to give up the hope that someone will finally know what a good person they are, that someone will give them the praise and love they needed as a child, that someone will listen to their fears and their side of the story.

And yet, at Step Two you give up that hope. You realize you have been trying to live your life as if you had received all that you needed as a child. And you filled in for what you didn't get by thinking there was something wrong with you. This is very difficult for people to understand. Robbie used to think that the way he treated his children was the right way. It didn't matter what the kids said, what his wife said. If it was good enough for him, then it was good enough for his kids. He changed by remembering just how empty of fatherly love his childhood had been. His self took Step Two by recognizing his need to love and be loved by his children—not to control them and run their lives as his father had done to him.

At Step Two you are no longer mad at or blame your past. Nor are you denying what really occurred. What happened or didn't happen in your past "was." It isn't any longer. You realize the past really happened, you realize what you missed in it, but now you have the present and the future to make happen what you want. It is exciting to know that from now on you are in control of your life. As you take control, you will suffer the separation anxiety of leaving your own past. *To pass through this stage successfully you must grieve and mourn for the life you lost when your self was controlled by your images.* You also grieve for the images that are losing control. The images were there to protect you in the past and now are useless. They have served their purpose and are no longer needed. At the same time you focus on the excitement of the future. You are both being born (the emerging self) and dying (loss of the images). Life is starting to become easier to live. Clients describe this in similar ways:

"I can catch my breath for the first time."
"My life seems easier somehow."
"Where have I been?"
"I have new horizons."
"I'm waking up for the first time in my life."
"I can fly, I have wings, I have been trapped for so long."
"I can see the light at the end of the tunnel."

For Shelly Step Two was very difficult. She didn't feel her best and she wasn't in control, and yet she didn't want to go back to Step One. She was in between. Learning to play the game of life, like learning anything new, requires the willingness and courage to go through the transition periods when the old behaviors are unacceptable and the new behaviors don't work. Shelly made the transition and found personal power. In the next chapter we'll find out about high performance.

COACH'S NOTES

1. Life has ultimate patience. It won't leave you behind. It will wait for you. It will renew itself for you. The only price of admission is to participate the best you can.
2. It is in vogue to "take responsibility." How can you do that if you don't know what responsibility is? But you do know what it feels like to be "you at your best." If you want to live with responsibility, then try to be your best. You don't have to succeed—simply try to accept what is.
3. Fear and power are cousins. Fear is held-in power. And yet power in action leads us into the unknown, beyond our images—therefore to fear's doorstep. If you are willing to exert your power in your life—and you reach the edge, the outer limit of what you know—let go and touch for a moment the immense power of the universe spread before you. Let go and let the universe play through you.

·24·

High Performance

In the preface I stated that this book was written for people who wanted to perform at their best. When you can perform at your best at will, when you are consistently good, when you have taken control, when you know how to use your personal power, when you greet your life with joy and exhilaration, when you love to push your limits and find out just how good you can be—you have taken the third step toward being in total sync. You know what high performance means. What about it? Is that what you want? If it is, then let's find out what the requirements are and then go for it.

Shelly reached a point where she had a new state of awareness, as distinct as sleep from waking. Except it was from waking to awareness. She said one day, "For the first time in my life I don't regret my life."

She began to experience personal power. She sensed her control over her life. She had learned to play her life as an athlete does. She was no longer controlled by her past, by her out-of-date images, or by other people's expectations. Instead, she knew what she needed and she could listen to what other people needed. She had personal power and she used it to live her life. She started standing up for herself and standing up to other people. She wasn't willing to let her images take control or let her self drift.

The more her self took control over her images, the less control her images had and the more effective they became. She used her images as tools. She knew what life zone she was in, what image was appropriate for that zone, and what needs she could fill. Her power came from knowing herself at her best. She had her inner gyroscope. Often Shelly was simultaneously scared and excited. And yet feeling scared or unsure did not keep her from moving forward in her life. Her life was no longer a mystery to her. She had developed a natural awareness.

Shelly was able to perform at high levels because she wasn't spending time getting over feeling bad. She learned that *high performance was not difficult* because she had eliminated her low points. High performance is impossible if you are spending your energy getting over the effects of your low points. Shelly had her cycle under her control and was in sync.

Step Three Checklist

1. You know what life zone you are in most of the time_____
2. You know what signals people are sending you _____
3. You know what signals you are sending other people_____
4. You know that your emotions are emotions and not the only reality_____
5. You know that your thoughts are your thoughts and merely your point of view_____
6. You are willing to stand up for what you know and feel without being rigid and attacking_____
7. You are no longer ticked off by the things that really used to get to you_____
8. You have an active inner awareness, which guides your behavior_____
9. You find it easy to love yourself and others and understand yourself and others_____
10. You find it difficult to blame yourself or others_____
11. You use your four questions_____
12. You consistently have a Player Attitude_____

What did you notice in this checklist? Remember to use the questions in this checklist as characteristics to strive for.

COACH'S EXERCISE

Take the time to ask yourself the following questions and answer them right now. What would be your probability of winning if you had this kind of cycle? What beliefs of yours would have to change? What expectations? How would your work life change? How would your love life change? Then just think about your answers. It is possible.

At Step Three Shelly found she could perform at high levels because she was no longer giving energy away to her images. She had the power to pay attention to the world, to cross her emotional frontiers, and to win in critical situations. If her husband was sending her image-signals to fight or to be a victim, she no longer responded to his image. Instead, she had the power to respond directly to her husband's self. She wasn't caught in her own or in anyone else's image traps. Her self was in control.

At Step Three, the self creates an army of images to serve it. You finally have a wardrobe of images so that you are in sync with the real world. You have images for work, for love, for health and sports, for family, for friends. Your self isn't forced to use the same old worn-out images day in and day out. The more choices your self has, the stronger it gets. The images no longer distort and deny. The emotional frontier is no longer difficult to penetrate. The belief systems are flexible and mature. You no longer expect yourself or anyone else to do anything but play the game of life. You are able to have those self-to-self connections with other people. And playing the game of life means you are willing to be a human being and let others be human. You don't have to judge yourself or others as if there were an ideal state.

COACH'S EXERCISE: How Do You Take Step Three?

---

1. Identify what you need.
2. Identify the zone that need can be filled in.

3. Create or use the image that effectively satisfies that need.

4. Give yourself the reward of the need satisfaction.

Shelly could do all four things to take Step Three. She was winning the game of life. Periodically she experienced Step Four. Let's find out what that was in the next chapter.

·25·

Imagelessness

I have found that as clients move through the first three steps they develop what seems to be a natural mysticism. What was at first for them the game of life becomes the art of life and, finally, the realization of life. This awareness softens them, makes them introspective and outgoing at the same time. They are able to be deep within themselves while reaching out to participate fully in the world. They find a new understanding of the world, of others, and of life continually evolving and expanding. At Step Four you find where you have come from—life itself.

Step Four Checklist

1. You are doing something and you have a sense of timelessness. You are in the here and now _____
2. You have a sense of unity with the world _____
3. You know you are doing the best that you can at the moment. You feel free of the outcome _____
4. You have a profound sense of self-love _____
5. You have a powerful sense of loving someone else _____
6. You have the dual awareness of the delight of being alive and the reality of your own vulnerability _____
7. You see the suffering and the joy of the people around you _____
8. You understand just how minuscule your understanding really is _____

9. You know you belong in the universe _____
10. You sense that you are not your own creation_____

Think of these questions as forms of meditations. Read them and understand them and then use them to help you understand what Step Four is like.

Step Four is the bliss of being human. It is the state of awareness in which compassion, altruism, and love flourish. When you are at Step Four you are able to care, to teach, and to do for others, and from your doing you get great satisfaction. There is only the sense of unity, peace, and harmony with life. You perceive the world directly without your images. At Step Four there is a completeness to life. Finally, you take your place in life. You have a role to play, and that is to live. You are no longer half living and half waiting for someone to save you. You become the prime mover in your life. The serenity of Step Four allows you to penetrate to the self of other people and keeps you from falling into image traps of other people or of the culture.

Step Four is just the self responding naturally to the world. There are different times when each person reaches Step Four. Step Four is not a place; it is a state of being or expanded awareness, which comes and goes naturally. At Step Four you are able to make the self-to-world connection that gives you the sense of where you have come from and where you are going. It is also the source of knowing what to do in the present—because Step Four gives you perspective without image distortion.

As your self becomes stronger and stronger this state comes more often, but it is not a state that you can work toward. There is no "mystic capitalism"—you don't win something for Step Four. It is the experience of knowing that you are alive and there is nothing to lose and nothing to gain. At this step you live your life for the good of life. Most people can't think of themselves as ever reaching this state of being. And yet it is occurring within each one of us all the time. It is not a state to gain but one to stop losing. You are filled with power and you have stopped the leaks.

COACH'S EXERCISE: HOW DO YOU TAKE STEP FOUR?

You don't take Step Four. It is the natural consequence of taking the first three steps. It is not something you strive for; it is an experience that will come from your self.

Shelly had moments when she took Step Four and then she would go back to Step Three. At Step Four you begin to understand life, yourself, and other people from the crystal clarity of imagelessness. It is what the philosopher Martin Buber described as I-Thou. There is a mutuality between self and others, inner and outer. There is no judgment at Step Four. There is only understanding and experience.

We are almost finished with this book: It is just the beginning for all of us. We started with the attitude of playing life as a game and now we come to the philosophy—the pragmatics of reality.

COACH'S NOTES

1. What is out there in the unknown? The infinite. At least bigger than you and I and all the telescopes can fathom. But whatever is out there gave rise to what is here. If you discover your own personal synchrony you hear the whole universe singing to you.
2. Play the game of life with passion. Let yourself get swept up into the game of your life—kiss the lips, raise the children, love the lovers, and try, beyond whatever you thought you could be, to be your best.
3. When is life mysterious? If I am here and doing the most that I can, and then I realize how big the world is, how individual each person is, that I didn't create the world, then I can relax. All I can do is the best that I can at this moment; I can't control what or who is outside of me. This gives me a sense of place in the universe. I am right here. My role in life is very simple—to live.

CHAPTER

·26·

The Pragmatics of the Game of Life

T he pragmatics of the game of life are the opposite of
perfection. We live in a culture that idolizes perfection. We are addicted to perfection. We are swimming in the
illusions of perfection. We think life should be this or that rather
than how life actually is. Perfection is the context used by many
people who spend time judging themselves and others. If you
believe in perfection, then you haven't figured out that you are
finite and highly imperfect. Perfection exists within the context
of the infinite. We are finite beings and what we have is the joy of
doing the best we can. Perfection means you know the past, the
present, and the future simultaneously, and that is only possible if
you are infinite. For many people the need for perfection is a
denial of their mortality. They fear death because they have not
lived as fully as they can.

In the game of life the pragmatics are very simple—you play
the game and learn. Each time you play you learn more. You
learn by finding the options that work, by not pretending that
you are going to be a "perfect" person always choosing the perfect option. Instead, you are doing the best you can. And in doing
the best you can, you will make mistakes and come face to face
with the simple fact that you are human. And that your humanity
is quite enough.

It is very hard to admit that you have done the best you could,
especially when you look back over your life and realize just how
much your images have distorted your perceptions, thoughts,

and feelings. You realize that because of the distortion you have made mistakes, hurt other people, and hurt yourself. And yet it has to be all right because in each of those circumstances, which in hindsight were mistakes, you were trying to do the best you could. This is so difficult to do—to forgive ourselves for being human beings, for not being perfect. But that is what it means to be a human being. To be human is to be perfectly imperfect.

There are people who come to see me who have been abused, hurt, and damaged. For these people the first step is healing. Human beings, given support and motivation, have an incredible ability to heal themselves. But even while they are healing they are playing. They are not sick. They are not patients. They are injured life-athletes. Once they have healed, they move on to what Shelly learned. If the context for Shelly had been that she was "sick," then she would have had to get over being sick. The sick context would have defined her game for her. But the pragmatics of Shelly's life were that she was not sick, neurotic, or helpless but that she needed coaching because she wanted something more. She wanted to live her life in a way that was more satisfying.

In the game of life the context is playing. And as you learn to play, you are remembering what you have forgotten. You do know how to play. You have played. As you play you learn to live with more and more intensity. And as your intensity grows, you will no longer be the person you once were. You will become the person you are now. You will become the adult who is detached from the illusions of perfection, you will become detached from the games of the images, and you will feel a commitment to do whatever you do at "your best."

The pragmatics are that the game is never over until your life is over. As you become an expert in playing the game of life, life becomes more fun. But to become an expert requires the same time and the same conditioning your body requires. Your personality, like your body, can be exercised and strengthened so that you can play the game of life and win. Being happy and effective is challenging because it takes you into the unknown of your life. It is actually much easier to get over a problem than to play the game of life because of the existence of the unknown.

But it is in that unknown that your life will unfold. And the more your life unfolds the more you begin to see your thoughts as nothing more than tools, and your emotions as wondrous gifts, and your actions as expressions of your life. You will have taken control. In the game of life you determine what you will do. When you are *not* playing the game of life, you believe you are defined by your problems.

The game of life is quite simple. You take control by recognizing that what is doesn't necessarily have to be. You have choice, and power to act on your choices. *Recognition is the birth of consciousness.* You don't have to do anything. The human machine is built to do it naturally. Just allow your self to be aware. It is time now for you to play. You will find that you deserve the best: "You at your best." You are ready to play the game of life. You are learning to learn, changing in a changing world, and taking control in order to more fully let go. Play.

More Information About Personal Coaching

Life Zones, like all the other books Dr. Corriere has written, reflects his continuing interest in helping people perform at their best, experience less stress, and more effectively play the game of life. Additional information on applying the principles of *Life Zones* for personal and business use is available through

Personal Coaching Institute
P.O. Box 1247
Aspen, Colorado 81612

Source Notes

Chapter Two

C. Argyris and D. Schon, *Theory in Practice: Increasing Professional Effectiveness* (San Francisco: Jossey-Bass, Inc., 1974).

C. Argyris and D. Schon, *Organizational Learning: A Theory of Action Perspective* (Menlo Park, Calif.: Addison-Wesley Publishing Company, 1978).

E. J. Langer and J. Rodin, "The Effects of Choice and Enhanced Personal Responsibility for the Aged: A Field Experiment in an Institutional Setting," *Journal of Personality and Social Psychology,* 35(12), 1977.

Lisa Hunter, *Friends Can Be Good Medicine: A Resource Guide* (California Department of Mental Health, 1982).

Chapter Three

Lisa Hunter, *Friends Can Be Good Medicine: A Resource Guide* (California Department of Mental Health, 1982).

George Vaillant, *Adaptation to Life* (New York: Little, Brown and Company, 1977).

Norman Bradburn, *The Structure of Psychological Well-Being* (Chicago: Aldine Publishing Company, 1969).

Source Notes

Chapter Four

Edward Hall, *This Hidden Dimension* (New York: McGraw-Hill, 1976).

Chapter Eleven

H. Selye, *The Stress of Life* (New York: McGraw-Hill, 1976).

Chapter Sixteen

G. A. Kelly, *The Psychology of Personal Constructs* (New York: Norton, 1955).

Chapter Twenty-one

B. Russell and T. Branch, *Second Wind* (New York: Random House, 1979).
Covert Bailey, *Fit or Fat* (New York. Houghton Mifflin, 1978).

Index

Index

winning:
  attitude vs. talent in, 117
  benefits of, 171
  losing vs., 23, 80–81
  in Personal Zone, 87
  Player Attitude and, 31, 49
  rules for, 22, 47, 81, 82
Wooden, John, 224
work:
  attitude toward, 37, 53, 62, 67, 80
  communicating at, 76, 80
  Player Attitude and, 41, 49, 62, 83
  play vs., 37
  relationships at, 49, 76
  self-esteem at, 80
  in Social Zone, 80–81, 88, 168–169

  and stress, 79
  success in, 76, 79, 80
worry, 43, 148
worthlessness, feelings of, 150, 153

"you at your best":
  as guide to success, 109, 110, 124
  and image-making, 131–133, 162–163, 185, 187
  maintaining of, 113, 128
  as model, 42, 109, 110, 111, 113, 120, 124
  performing at, 69, 81, 82, 124, 157
  play and, 37, 81, 124
  responsibility for, 41, 120
  synchrony and, 108

About the Authors

D r. Richard Corriere has authored five other books, among them *Psychological Fitness*. Based in Aspen, Colorado, and New York City, he works as a consultant, to help individuals and corporations nationwide use his personal coaching method.

Patrick M. McGrady, Jr., is coauthor of the best-selling *The Pritikin Program for Diet and Exercise* and author of *The Youth Doctors* and *The Love Doctors*. He is currently director for CAN-HELP (a cancer-patient referral and information service) and has appeared on over five hundred television and radio talk shows. He lives in Port Ludlow, Washington.